Protocol Handbook
for the Leather Slave:
Theory and Practice

Protocol Handbook
for the Leather Slave:
Theory and Practice

An M/s Studies Book
Published by The Nazca Plains Corporation
Las Vegas, Nevada
2008

ISBN: 1-887895-15-9

Published by

The Nazca Plains Corporation ®
4640 Paradise Rd, Suite 141
Las Vegas, NV 89109-8000

Layout Editor, Blake Stevens
Art Direction, Robert Steele
Photography by Corwin
www.photosbycorwin.com

Dedication

Foremost, this book is dedicated to Mistress,
For she has trusted and embraced my Vision,
Thus enabling me even to See this Road.

Next, this book is dedicated to my slave
For she has taken gigantic personal and
Emotional risks to serve me in this Lifestyle.

So, this book is for them, for together
Mistress and my slave have joined me
On my walk down The Road Less Traveled,
And that has made all the difference.

The Road Not Taken

Two roads diverged in a yellow wood,
And sorry I could not travel both
And be one traveler, long I stood
And looked down one as far as I could
To where it bent in the undergrowth;

Then took the other, just as fair,
And having perhaps the better claim
Because it was grassy and wanted wear,
Though as for that the passing there
Had worn them really about the same,

And both that morning equally lay
In leaves no step had trodden black.
Oh, I marked the first for another day!
Yet knowing how way leads on to way
I doubted if I should ever come back.

I shall be telling this with a sigh
Somewhere ages and ages hence:
Two roads diverged in a wood, and I,
I took the one less traveled by,

And that has made all the difference.

Robert Frost

Acknowledgments

I particularly wish to thank three established Leather Masters for allowing me to use their own Protocols as the basis for what has now become this book. My first exposure to Leather Protocols came from Officer Wes, one of my good friends when he lived in Austin and one of my mentors when I went through the Austin Mentors' Program. I see him now once or twice a year at Leather conferences, and still feel very close to him. I also thank the Good Officer for his careful and thoughtful reading of an early draft of this book. He made a number of good catches, particularly concerning aspects of the concept and application of the Mater/slave dynamic.

I have also been heavily influenced by Master Steve Sampson – personally, and also by his Butchmann's Academy website (now APEX – Arizona Power Exchange; see citation on the References page at the end of the book). Here, a wealth of well-organized material formed important parts of my *Manual of Protocol* and lives on in parts of Chapters 1-4 of this book. Over the ensuing years, I have been drawn to Master Steve, and I make a point of attending his presentations at Leather conferences. We see one another perhaps two times a year.

Finally, a local Leather Master, Master Gary McEntyre, was kind enough to give me a copy of his own Protocol Manual. Many times, I have watched the exquisite public protocols that Master Gary has taught his boy tommy, and it prompted me to ask him if he would share his personal Protocol Manual with me. He did so, and I found many sections in that document that felt exactly right to me. Again, these have been included, here, in their adapted form – principally in chapters 1 and 2.

Thanks to the three of you. You have made a HUGE difference in my life.

In addition to recognizing those who helped to provide the impetus for this book and the initial editing, I wish to acknowledge two people for their particular service. First, I thank slave mindi for preparing the "Courtesan Services" section and also for reading this draft both for *content edit* and for *line edit,* thus catching numerous places that needed fleshing out. Second, I thank Susan from San Antonio for doing such an outstanding job writing the section on boot and leather care. One look at Charles' boots and I knew I'd found the author for that section.

Special thanks to koura, who did extensive, detailed editing to an early draft of this opus. Thanks to her, readers have a much "smoother" work in their hands.

Robert J. Rubel

Contents

Protocol Handbook
for the Leather Slave:
Theory and Practice

By Robert J. Rubel, PhD

Preface

Most people have at least one passion. It may be origami, sports, gardening or reading. Master/slave protocols are my passion. This is my manual, and if it helps you to create your own protocol manual, I freely offer it to you.

First and foremost, this is a book written for people who know something about relationships based on Dominance and submission – the BDSM (**B**ondage, **D**iscipline, **S**ado**M**asochism) Lifestyle. If you lack experience in this lifestyle, chances are that you will also lack the context necessary to understand many of its subtleties, as presented in this book. There is really no way around that. But if you DO have experience in power exchange and/or authority exchange, this book is for you.

This book began as a training guide for my own slave. I needed a way to explain ways I wished my slave to stand, to sit and to speak, as well as ways to please me as the slave's "Master" in a consensual "Master/slave" (M/s) relationship.

So, "Why?" you might ask: "Why should I read this book? Why should I be concerned with protocols, neat homes, and elegant meal-service? Why should I care about the lighting in my living room and whether or not there are candles on the dining room table? Why should I care about ways I want my slave to do things?"

The answer, as Larry Townsend so aptly put it in his landmark book, *The Leatherman's Handbook* (1972), is that "erotic sensation is never limited strictly to the genital areas; it involves the entire body, utilizing those parts which may have no sexual significance under other circumstances."

So, take the thought that you're setting out on a path of providing *total sensory pleasure,* and marry it to the world of Leather, the world of power exchange (Master/slave relations) and you have an environment in which the Master/Mistress/Dom/Domme has the capacity and power to create a sensual/sexual fantasy world of his/her own making.

(Note: I will discuss the difference between *Master* and *Dom* later in the book; overall, I will use Master and Dom in a gender-neutral way. That is, rather than clutter the text with Master/Mistress and Dom/Domme I will simply use Master and Dom. No slight is in any way intended towards female Masters or FemDommes. The Protocols described here can be applied whether the Master is male or female and whether the slave is male or female.

To the extent that you want others around you to support the world you create, you need to be able clearly to define what you seek. For example, if your goal is to obtain *consistently outstanding sexual performance* from your slave, it may help to create a context for the relationship that is sexually charged and "special." If your goal is to obtain *consistently outstanding personal service* from your slave, it may help if you create a context for the relationship that is based on the use of specialized and finely-honed service.

So, while on the surface this is a book about *protocols* and *rituals* – it's really about creating the environment, the milieu, that leads to hours of outrageous Leathersex.

Well, that's a good part of it, at any rate. As Guy Baldwin points out, the other half of the equation concerns *transformance.* He notes that the very palpable power underlying Master/slave dynamics is that through the Master/slave (M/s) lifestyle, we enable our slave(s) to let go of their old life and help them build new beliefs. As I write this book in 2006, my slave is hardly recognizable in behavior, outlook and appearance to the person who petitioned to be my slave in the summer of 2003.

I hope you enjoy reading this book as much as I've enjoyed the path it took to get to the place that I could write it.

Introduction

Before we Get Started – Critical Information

This book is the gender-neutral version of Protocols: Handbook for the Female slave. If you have that book, do NOT buy this book. The only difference between the books is that this book is gender-neutral and the other book assumes that the slave is female.

This book is intended to demonstrate ways that a modern-day slave can serve his or her Master. This book is intended for those in the M/s lifestyle for whom devotion to the Master is expressed through obedience and service.

Slave collars are a visible symbol of the relationship between the Master and the slave. Many M/s relationships start out with a *training collar.* Other than a temporary *collar of protection,* the training collar is often the first leather collar offered by a Master to a potential slave. After a training collar, many relationships proceed to a *collar of consideration* (indicating a deepening relationship) before a *full collar* is offered. A full collar signifies a permanent relationship.

When entering into a Master/slave relationship, one "hot topic" concerns the slave's training. In our case, as we proceeded, training grew deeper and broader. What began as *protocol training* for our public appearances at Leather events grew to include protocols for daily life. Pretty soon the slave learned how to prepare my breakfast, lunch and dinner. And, as you will soon read, preparing my kind of *dinner* requires significant attention to detail.

So, I began to write it all down so my slave could keep it straight – and now you're holding the result in your hands.

In reality, this is a very detailed manual of **How I Want my Partner to Behave**. Of course, outside of the world of *Internal Enslavement,* as this practice is sometimes called, this book would be a laughable male pipe dream, the Ultimate Male Fantasy. After all, who is going to approach a potential partner and ask: "Sir? How may I change my behavior better to please you, Sir?" Even if someone asked such a question, how many people can answer with more than generalities? While the content of this book is a little unusual in the world at-large, in the world of Leather BDSM Master/slave relations, this world of Protocols and Rituals, the contents of this book are quite real.

There is a key point to mention at the beginning of this book: my slave and I identify as "Leather." So, let me start by giving my own operating definition of *Leather* and *Not-Leather*. This is important because the Protocols presented in this book reflect a Leather perspective. If you have no experience of the Leather Lifestyle, these may be a bit confusing at best, and at worst, strike you as bizarre.

In a general way, the current and diverse "BDSM Community" has developed from two major *paths*. At the risk of over-simplifying these origins for the sake of brevity, the "Leather" path is an outgrowth of returning gay GIs from WWII who sometimes associated with motorcycle gangs in the 1950s and 1960s. They brought *hierarchy, spirituality* and *protocols* to modern-day practices. The other BDSM path, a path that I'll refer to as "Not-Leather," evolved seperately out of the swinging movement of the 1960s and before. The Leather path has greater focus on obedience, service, protocols, and spirituality, where as the Not-Leather path has more focus on amorous love.

Of course, these paths cross over at times; there are few absolutes, here. You'll see some of the protocols mentioned in this book practiced among Not-Leather kinksters. You'll find Leatherfolk who don't use many protocols. But, in a general sense, there are distinctions. The easiest way to experience the differences between these two BDSM paths is to attend both a "Leather" weekend conference (such as Southplains Leatherfest) and a "Not-Leather" weekend conference (such as Beat me in St Louis). "How can you spot the differences?" you ask. Well, for starters, are there predominantly gay couples walking around? Are most of the attendees wearing leather vests with "run pins" covering them? If yes, you're at a Leather event.

The Leather-BDSM Lifestyle is about Obedience and Service. As wonderwoman wrote in volume I number 1 of the e-zine *Simply Service*, "Obedience is the process of aligning one's behavior with the expectations of another. In a Master/slave relationship, this translates into the process of the slave learning to align her behavior with the expectations of her Master. Obedience is an outward expression of the slave's ability to integrate her trust in and respect for her Master and her belief that he not only knows her well enough to know her best interests, but that he also loves her enough to consistently act on them." That definition is so accurate that I cannot improve upon it.

One of the best articles I've read on the uniqueness of the Leather culture was written by Steve Elliott for a competition that Jack Rinella held back in 2003 (Steve's article took third place). Here, Elliott wrote that those within the Leather culture share four traits in varying degrees: attire, sexuality, community and spirit.

> **Attire** – a strong tendency towards wearing *black*. At Leather gatherings, that might look like black jeans, black "Sam Brown" belt, paratrooper boots, black T-shirt and black vest – with or without "run pins" – and boots. At more formal Leather events, spit-polished paratrooper boots, black leather pants, etc.

> **Sexuality** – There are a number of books in print about Leathersex. As Elliott points out, it's fundamentally about headspace, power exchange and using the senses – all five of the senses. As Elliott puts it, Leathersex is about "...the feel of cold restraints, the smell of sweat, the taste of another's armpit, the sound of a flogger, the look of the leather harness framing a torso." Leathersex involves a more intense level of *connection* than is commonly found in "vanilla" sex ("vanilla" is the term used to denote those who are "not-kinky," who are not within the BDSM community. Thus "vanilla sex" refers to "standard intercourse as practiced by those outside the BDSM community"). In the Leather world, a person must be in closer touch with oneself and one's partner(s).

> **Community** – Many people who enter the BDSM world tend to drop out of the "vanilla" world and to socialize almost exclusively with others from the BDSM Community. Elliott points

out that this is one of the defining characteristics of Leatherfolk – a tendency to socialize with others of like mind. We go to meetings and play parties with others who share our Leather orientation.

Leather Spirit – Elliott notes that "Leather spirit" transcends attire, sexuality, and community. It's the "spiritual core" of this form of BDSM. I don't want to spend a great deal of time on this, but I'll make a brief observation. It is my experience that when Leatherfolk "play," the *tools* (whips, floggers, etc.) are the *vehicles* to take the person *receiving the action* (called the "bottom" as well as the person *administering the action* (called the Top) to a different plane – often with cathartic consequences. In the Not-Leather world, my sense (particularly among those who have been involved only for a few years) is that a flogging is a flogging. A spanking is a spanking: WYSIWYG "what-you-see-is-what-you-get."

By way of summary, one of the often-repeated mythologies is how the heterosexual BDSM community grew out of the Gay Leather culture. That mythology is not exactly accurate. Robert Bienvenu, in his doctoral dissertation on the origins of BDSM both in Europe and in the US (www.americanfetish.net), reports that there were historically two cultures in the US – gay and heterosexual. The swinging community gave the heterosexual ("het") SM culture (which was well in place long before the 60s) additional means of contacting one another. However, neither the gay nor the het culture knew about the other, and each developed in different ways. Thus, many Leathermen thought (and still think) they were the origin of it all. (Thanks to Master Bert Cutler for bringing Dr. Bienvenu's work to my attention.)

Because of these different beginnings, the "feel" of these two BDSM cultures is quite different – though both cultures are now somewhat pansexual. In the broadest sense, the Leather BDSM culture has a structure, formality and spirituality that is largely absent from the Not-Leather BDSM culture.

––––––––

To give you a robust feel for this Lifestyle, I have endeavored to combine fact, philosophy, pragmatism and commentary. In most cases, after I provide the protocol, I will comment on why that protocol is the way it is. These notes are intended to help those who want better to understand this M/s subculture.

This work began as my personal *Manual of Protocol* for my slave. One day when I was working on this project, a senior Leatherman happened to be at my home. We started talking about my *Manual*. He noted that Masters frequently don't know exactly HOW they want to be served and that he knew of no current book that addressed this issue. Furthermore, he thought this broad treatment would be a valuable addition to the Leather literature. (He also commented that most slaves would probably appreciate some guidance about the more formal service covered in this book, better to please their Masters.) After more discussion, He suggested that I convert my Manual of Protocol into a book format for others to use. Ultimately, I agreed to do that and you're holding the result in your hands.

What This Book Is

As I've said, this book began as my own personal *Manual of Protocol* for my own slave. I've now converted it to a *handbook* that is more generally applicable to others. This book shows how you can create your own protocols to guide your slave's behavior, whether or not they are in your presence.

Often, those fairly new to BDSM have a vague sense that M/s relationships are somehow *better than* D/s relationships and in a universe different from Top/bottom play. That is not so; it's just that your slave is *different*.

As Master Skip Chasey points out, Top/bottom play is about the physical body, Dominant/submissive play is about the mental body and Master/slave relationships are about the spiritual body. Master Steve Sampson cuts it slightly differently: "Top and bottom play is about the *sexual self*; dominance and submission is about *energy* and Master/slave relationships are about the *spiritual*."

As **obedience** and **service** are at the core of the Master/slave dynamic, *protocols* become the means by which the slave aligns himself with Master's choices for personal service. In that light, each Master has to create protocols that enable his slave to express obedience through tailored service. "slave training" is all about teaching the slave to perform that service.

There is a great deal of fantasy built up about Master/slave relations, particularly about slave training. Often, these fantasies have something to do with, "Do what I say, or I'll punish you." That line of thought is foreign to me. Slaves are people – vibrant and intelligent people. While your slave's primary purpose is to serve you, your role, as Master, is to make sure that training is appropriate, relevant and complete. It's a long process, but as those of you know who have owned slaves in the past, the result is likely to be that those who knew your slave in earlier times now find a vastly changed person.

My method of training – true, long-term behavior modification – rests on reinforcing positive behaviors and downplaying the glitches. I recommend that you approach *slave training* in this way because if you repeatedly pick on little glitches, you risk conditioning your slave to be hypercritical and anxious when around you. Thus, I suggest that you not punish your slave for lapses in protocol – use the lapses as opportunities to discuss what was not pleasing and figure out how the experience can be more pleasing in the future.

So, why do I open this book with these paragraphs? I open it this way because this is a book written from my heart about a real, live, ongoing, dynamic Master/slave relationship. This is not a fantasy. M/s fantasies are very different from actuality. Living together in a 24/7 M/s relationship takes daily work. This takes daily practice. This takes commitment to the road less traveled.

Far more than a book of Protocols, this book presents a look into the BDSM **Leather** subculture as a whole. I have provided a *Commentary* after most of the protocols in order to relate them to the larger Purpose of the described activity. That is, the *Commentary* explains the "why" of the Protocol.

Absent the commentaries, this book instructs my slave how to behave in public and how to serve me in private. Everything in this book is actively used in my relationship with my slave.

This gives me a good way to transition to the next idea: There are many, many ways to approach Master/slave (M/s) relationships. Ultimately, a couple must develop protocols and rituals that support *who they are*. This book describes a range of protocols that you can adapt as you see fit for your own slave. It is not intended to be the final word on *protocols* for any other M/s relationship; there is no such thing as the "final word" about protocols.

Because I am somewhat intense and "driven" in my life, the protocols in this book reflect that personality. The level of detail I present may be a bit extreme for your situation – it might get in the way of your relationship. Then again, you may prefer even more rigor and detail in your lives than I've expressed in this book.

By way of summary, then, this book describes an approach to the way you and your slave may choose to be together as an outgrowth of who the two of you are in the world.

What This Book is NOT

First, this book is not about your **Contract**. Your Contract defines the terms and conditions of your *relationship* with your slave. This book defines the slave's *behavior*.

Second, this book of personal protocols is not fully generalizable. That is, you – the reader – are not likely to want the same out of your slave that I want from my slave, so some of these protocols will not sing to you. However, this material should give you ideas to help you design your own Protocol Manual.

This book does NOT purport to represent any other Masters' protocols or rituals for their slaves. There are as many ways of approaching an M/s relationship as there are people practicing these activities. Guy Baldwin, in <u>Ties that Bind</u>, observes: "I have seen a Master with several slaves. Some slaves have more than one Master. Some slaves have slaves, and some Masters are themselves slaves to yet other Masters. Another slave I know has a lover (mostly vanilla) and a Master as well..." Personally, I know of an instance where the slave's Owner and the slave's Master are different people; the slave has been allowed a Master for a particular purpose.

This book presents beliefs, activities and behaviors that fit *who we are* as people and as a couple. There are many Paths within this Lifestyle. You, as a Master, must select your own. Oh, and this is not a manual that explains how we behave with our biological families. There, we match our behavior to the standards of the family member present, especially in regards to minors.

And this is a Leather book – it may or may not *resonate* with you. The tone and temper of this book reflects the highly structured Leather culture in which I feel at home. A Not-Leather BDSM Master/slave relationship is likely to be quite different. And, of course, there are other models, such as the Gorean M/s model, about which I know nothing beyond whispers and innuendos.

Definitions: Etiquette, Protocol and Ritual

Etiquette represents a set of rules that guide us toward the polite way of interacting with others in the world. Etiquette is culture-bound and situation-bound. For example, you can imagine that "proper etiquette" among inmates in a U.S. Federal prison is a world apart from "proper etiquette" among students of a private British boarding school. At its core, *etiquette* represents a way of showing respect toward others while demonstrating your understanding of good manners.

Protocols represent a set of rules that govern specific actions or behavior in a particular situation. So – there is a "lockdown protocol" in prison and a "test-taking protocol" in the boarding school.

In terms of our BDSM lifestyle "etiquette" can be said to be *outward looking* – it's describing the way you interact with others within our culture. "Protocols," however, are *inward looking;* they describe the way the Master wishes his/her slave to do specific things within the M/s structure. Protocols enhance our play and relationships with structure, ritual and symbols.

Rituals are like tradition – ways that we choose to do things that are repeated with some regularity, but without a set of rules that govern specific behavior. For example, when it's cool enough outside to have a fire in the fireplace, my evening ritual is to have appetizers and a drink with my slave in front of the fireplace while listening to scene music. It's not a protocol; it's a ritual. But, there are many little protocols that direct how my slave prepares the living room for our appetizers and then serves them to me.

How Protocols Come to Be

Protocols are an outgrowth of a Master's values combined with Master's personal tastes and sense of style.

A Master who most values honesty and integrity may create protocols focused on these. A Master who values sitting in front of a television drinking beer and eating popcorn may develop protocols about the temperature of the beer, how it's served to him and how the popcorn comes to be placed beside him.

The things that I, personally, value will become crystal clear as you read this book. But, that doesn't mean that YOU will value them or be interested in the protocols I've built around them. The best I can offer are solid examples of internally congruous protocols that you can actually use with your slave.

Masters, after all, are Eagles. They build their own worlds; they don't flock to emulate worlds created by others.

Why Use Protocols

So, "Why use protocols?"

First, to use business-speak, protocols turn routine actions into *defined, repeatable events*. It's like going to a franchised restaurant: whether you're in Los Angeles or Boston, the food preparation and presentation will be virtually identical. Similarly, when I ask my slave to do something for me, I can be assured that the action will be executed according to our protocols regardless of the circumstances surrounding my request. I can relax and not concern myself about how my slave will act/react. Because I've written out and taught my slave how to behave in most common situations, I'm no longer concerned about having to micromanage. This frees me and enables me to relax around the slave in ways that have seldom been possible in non-M/s relationships.

Second, protocols focus the mind and declare our mutual **intention** to be fully present – body, mind and spirit – for what is about to take place, and to clearly declare that intention through stylized action.

Third, protocols make a relationship **special**. "Protocols in action" communicate to the other person – and to anyone watching – just how valued your relationship is. One of the reasons this book presents such *formal* protocols is because it stresses this point: in my world, dinner is not just a time to eat food, it's a time to celebrate the uniqueness of my relationship with my slave.

I am reminded of the 2004 motion picture *50 First Dates* with Adam Sandler and Drew Barrymore. The female character (Lucy Whitmore) had been in a car accident with the result that her memory self-erased every 24 hours. The male character, Henry Roth, set out on a mission to make Lucy fall in love with him anew every single day – for every single day was a new meeting for Lucy. In my M/s relationship with my slave, I fall in love again every single night – when my slave comes to me Dressed and in High Protocol. It's magic. It's like nothing else I've ever experienced – and happens night after night.

How this Book is Constructed

About the Writing Style

A brief word about writing style: I'm an educational sociologist by training. Within my specialty, I've published two academic books and over 30 articles for professional journals. Traditionally, these tomes are written in third-person, passive voice and tend to put people to sleep. I'm not going to subject non-academic readers to this style. So, I'm writing this in first-person active voice; when I write a "commentary," I'm speaking directly to you.

About the Use of Capitals

Oh – and I LOVE A.A. Milne's *Winnie the Pooh* books and will sometimes Capitalize Odd Words by way of applying Emphasis. It's harmless. Having started my career as a high school English teacher, I know that I can get away with it.

About Chapter One

Chapter One sets the *context for slavery*. This is critical material, for it helps ensure that YOU and YOUR slave share common understandings about the M/s dynamic. Not all readers will agree with what I have written and that is somewhat beside the point. My point is that it just makes sense for each Master to consider the context in which the relationship should develop, refining and discussing this with his/her slave before advancing too far into the *relationship* that precedes the definition and use of *protocols*.

> **Commentary**: *This paragraph contains a "sleeper." Let me draw attention to the last line, above;* **relationship precedes protocols**.
>
> *In my experience, a Dom will sometimes start M/s negotiations with a person* **before he has spent time to establish their mutual desire to form a basic relationship.** *When the Dom starts right in with M/s negotiations without knowing the candidate very well, these negotiations often crater – or the relationship begins, but the slave gets released early from the training contract.*
>
> *A defining difference between "Leather" and "Not-Leather" is that in the* **Leather world**, *the slave usually petitions the Master, not the other way around. Through his demonstrable mastery and public service, the Master attracts slave candidates. Typically, the Leather Master will ask the slave candidate what the slave brings to the table – what the slave candidate knows or can do that will benefit the Master. These are threshold questions. The couple must establish that they WANT an M/s relationship – and to do that, they must spend time getting to know one another. If there's a fit, the couple can then begin more detailed negotiations about entering into a training contract. (See sample in Appendix A)*

An M/s Studies Book

Chapter 1

Common Understandings in Common Settings

Core Concepts of M/s Relations

In an M/s relationship, the Master consensually owns the slave in a manner not too unlike the way he owns a cherished pet. With the acceptance of a permanent collar, the slave enters into an exchange of *total obedience and service* on the slave's part in return for total responsibility for the slave's *emotional, physical, social, spiritual and financial well-being* on the Owner/Master's part. *(That's why this form of relationship is also referred to as TPE – Total Power Exchange.)*

This section expresses *how* the slave will learn the required level of obedience and service.

As with all areas of mastery, the SLAVE'S mastery is based upon:

- Consistency
- Focus
- Mindset

Through *consistent use,* the protocols in this book are intended – through *focus* – *to* produce the *mindset* you seek in your slave.

The Nature of Your Relationship

You may want to put some thought into defining the nature of your own relationship with your slave. For example, your slave performs *services* in return for receiveing *structure, security and direction* from you. But there may be more to it, in your case, so you have to think about it.

You also may wish to think through how you are going to introduce your slave to others *outside* the BDSM community. For example, you might consider referring to your slave as your "Personal Assistant." A *personal assistant* combines the skills of a butler plus executive secretary and valet. Personally, I find that to be a good description of my own slave.

In the context of a *personal assistant*, the slave is to gain such skills as to be able to provide:

- Formal personal service at table and throughout the day.
- Personal support for business activities.
- Complete household management.
- Sexual pleasure orally, anally and manually.
- Evening entertainment pleasure through music, dancing, or reading aloud.
- Visual pleasure through the slave's physical appearance both clothed and naked.

> *Commentary*: So – what's going on, here? And what does the slave get out of it? I've already alluded to Master's responsibilities, covered later in more detail. Right now, my purpose is to let the slave know what I expect out of OUR relationship. This is a "make-it or break-it" moment. This is when you set forth what it is that you are seeking in a slave – this is your "position statement."

Distinction between *Master* as an adjective and *Master* as a noun

Master (adj): a Leatherman who has earned such respect within the Community that other senior Leathermen refer to this person as a Master (regardless of gender). This respect is generally granted after years of selfless contribution to the Leather Community as a whole. This is an earned title that is usually granted in a public ceremony.

Master (n): Man or woman who seeks to exert total control over another. Typically, the Master and slave negotiate a contract that governs the duties and responsibilities of each person in this relationship. One of the *hot topics* engages the question as to whether or not a person can be a Master unless they have a slave – someone who actually *calls* the person "Master." I'll sidestep that embroilment for the moment, please. The issue, here, is whether the person wishes to play in the world of *authority exchange* rather than *power exchange* (discussed below). For our purposes, a Master takes *authority* over another either for a contracted period or permanently (more on this at a later point). A Master is a dominant who could occasionally bottom to someone else – this could be his own slave. In this sense, the Master is referred to as *versatile*. I'll distinguish between *Owner* and *Master* in the next section.

Distinction between *Owner* and *Master*
The term "Owner" is starting to be used to describe a permanent M/s relationship based on a simple exchange of profound vows. The Owner pledges to take care of all of the slave's needs and the slave pledges to obey and to serve his/her Owner. Period. Permanently. No contract. The key distinction between *Owner* and *Master* is the lack of a negotiated contract that usually forms the basis for the M/s relationship.

Distinction between *Master* and *Dom*
In my own experience, **Dom** is a role designation more commonly used in the "Not-Leather" world. One seldom – if ever – hears the term *Dom* used in the Leather world. The terms in the Leather world include: Master, Sir, Daddy and Top. "Dom" most frequently describes a psychological role that one person plays in relation to another in the general BDSM community.

Distinction between D/s and M/s
As Master Skip Chasey and Master Steve Sampson point out, D/s (Dominance and submission) is anchored in the mental body. D/s involves *power exchange* and is usually time-delimited. M/s is anchored in the spiritual body; M/s involves *authority exchange* and is a "way of being." Power exchange is used during a scene or during the time when the D/s couple is together; M/s is a lifestyle choice, and behaviors continue even when the Master and slave are not together. I will explain the power dynamics of these relationships in more detail below.

Commentary: This book has been written both for Leathermen and non-Leathermen. For that reason, some sentences will say: "...when the Master or Dom..." This is not a mistake: I identify as Leather, and in the traditional world of Leather, the term "Dom" is not generally used to refer to a Leatherman. This distinction is not intended as a "put-down," but simply to distinguish between the two approaches to BDSM.

The Nature of a slave

[As I mentioned in the preface, many ideas in this book came originally from material available from the Apex Academy/Butchmann's website, and are used here with permission. The next paragraphs are classic examples that I cannot improve upon.]

"A slave is a man or woman who has a special heart – a heart that requires a connection with another person in order to find completeness in their life. A person is born with slave heart – he cannot be 'made' into a slave nor can wishing to be one bring it about. It is a natural state. A slave may actualize their destiny by choosing to live in obedience to another person's will and to serve that person – their Master or Mistress – in obedience. Most slaves are very bright and capable, and they may make many decisions every day affecting other people, large sums of money, important projects, and so on. But slaves generally do not make decisions easily or well that concern themselves, and that is one of the reasons they seek a Master – to form that point of centered-ness from which to live their lives.

"Someone may have 'heart of slave' and be on a journey toward actualizing their destiny without yet having found the Master their heart tells them to give their life to. And others may feel drawn toward slavery but not yet know their hearts. For simplicity, all of the above will be referred to as 'slave' in this protocol.

"Once a slave truly understands that their existence is more complete and fulfilled in being obedient, everything else falls into place. A slave speaks in order to convey requested information or to request information about the Master's intentions. A slave eats, sleeps, washes, exercises, takes medication, and so on in order to remain healthy and available for service. slaves labor at tasks assigned by their Master or hold an outside job so that they can contribute to the Master's house-hold and not be a financial burden. Anything a slave is allowed to do for personal gratification is a gift from their Master, not a right. When this aspect of slave heart is realized, slaves start to find peace in their lives." (Butchmann's material: *What is a slave?*)

Distinction between Power Exchange/Authority Exchange

When the Dom accepts power from the submissive and the submissive gives up power to the Dom, this is referred to as a **power exchange**. When the submissive is away from the Dominant, he or she is free to resume control of his/her personal world. This is not so with **authority exchange**.

Authority exchange is the basis of an M/s (Master/slave) relationship. The slave permanently (or at least during the contract period) gives up authority over himself/herself to the Master. "What kind of author-ity?" you ask: the authority to make **willful** decisions. For example, depending upon the structure of the relationship, it can mean that the slave no longer controls decisions about how to use **time** or **money**. Authority does NOT change hands when the slave is out of Master's presence. This control is a core concept of the M/s dynamic and one of the reasons it is so crucial to delineate the boundaries of the rela-tionship during contract negotiations. **You get what you negotiate**. If the slave needs to maintain authority over a particular area of life, this must be spelled out in the contract before either the Master or slave can honestly enter the agreement. In the contract, you should always provide a means to renegotiate when unforeseen situations arise; this will make it easier for each of you to grow within the context of the relationship.

Who is this slave?

The slave is a person whose personal identity and sense of self is ful-filled through service and obedience to another person. To resonate in this relationship, the slave consents to give up extensive personal freedoms in exchange for extraordinary protection.

Now, the next question is: "Okay, but what *rights* does the slave have? While the answer depends upon your unique relationship, here's my shot at an answer.

1. The slave has certain (negotiated) rights regarding its biological family;

2. The slave has the right to bring to Master's attention an act he is about to do (or has done) that is illegal, unethical, or physically or emotionally abusive; and

3. The slave has the right to terminate and leave the relationship.

Beyond that, though, the slave has only those rights that have been granted by Master. The slave does not have the right to be upset by an order or Instruction. However, the slave has the right to ask for clarification, or to point out why that order or Instruction may not get the result Master seeks.

Again, while such practices vary between couples, the slave may not have the right even to prepare personal drinks or foods without first asking permission. In a general sense, the slave's whole reason for being is to make Master's life run more smoothly, ordered, and efficient. **To the extent that the slave's purpose in doing anything is personal and not for Master, that poses a direct conflict with the slave's reason for being.**

Now, don't lose track of the fact that Master is responsible for the slave's continuing growth and development. In that light, Master must temper what is asked of the slave, to ensure that it is — at heart — congruent with the goals and intentions of their M/s relationship.

The slave has no *prima fascia* right to make time demands of Master — but, it's hard to imagine a successful M/s relationship wherein Master largely ignores the slave's requests. That said, in a general sense, the slave has no personal time unless Master grants it.

This slave is NOT Master's "girlfriend." A "girlfriend" is a person with the same rights and responsibilities as her partner; the slave is property and has only those rights given her by her Master. A "girlfriend" might say: "Hey, I want to go see this movie. Let's go out to dinner and catch the show." The slave will say: "Master, if it pleases you,

Sir, there is a movie I think you would enjoy. May I have permission to describe it to you?"

> ***Commentary:*** *There is quite an active controversy within the M/s movement about the role of* love. *On the one hand, some Masters take the position that* love *contaminates the M/s dynamic because Master can never be sure whether the slave is complying with a request/Instruction out of love or out of obedience. Since obedience is the core of the M/s dynamic, Master would lose the capacity to monitor the slave's core reactions.*
>
> *On the flip side, many Masters feel that if they're going to put all the time and effort into training a slave with whom they will spend lots of time, they want to be submerged in a loving relationship with that person. But a loving relationship is not necessarily a girlfriend/boyfriend relationship, and the Master may want to carefully consider whether -- and how -- to suppress the tendency for slaves to think of their Master as their "girlfriend" or "boyfriend." "Girlfriend/boyfriend" relationships belong to the Vanilla World, and do not involve the authority or power exchanges inherent in D/s and M/s relationships.*
> *Also, there can be substantial differences between "the Master's love" and "the slave's love." The Master is more likely to love the slave than to be "in love" with the slave. However, the slave will probably "fall in love" with Master. It may be useful to discuss different forms of love with a prospective slave, lest they confuse your relationship.*

How is this slave to Think of himself/herself?

"A slave's reference to himself is understood to mean the part of his Master, or his Master's property, that consists of the slave's body, mind, and spirit. When a slave says (or writes) 'I,' it refers to the body and energies of the slave, but not his will, which as long as he is in service is obedient to that of his Master. When a slave says 'my' or 'mine,' it means that part of the Master's property that is in the slave's keeping or stewardship – except, of course, in the phrases 'my Master or Mistress,' 'my slave brother or sister,' or 'my slavery' (the only thing that truly belongs to a slave)." (Butchmann's: *Forms of Address*)

How Does this slave Fit into our Family Structure

If your Family is comprised of yourself and your slave, then the fit is straightforward. However, many Masters have complex and often polyamorous Households. You will have to develop your protocols to cover these particular arrangements.

Similarly, you will need protocols for your slave if another man or woman is present who is not of the Leather culture. In some cases, your protocol may call for your slave to serve you, as Master, but **not to serve** this other man or woman. This other person may serve him or herself or may be served by Master, as proper decorum dictates.

If another Leatherslave is present and participating with you in a Leather scene involving an evening meal, then you may instruct your slave to take on Alpha Slave responsibilities and instruct the visiting Leatherslave to serve you through your slave. Later, in the "Dining Protocols" section of this book, I explain the use of "Order of Precedence" charts that are a tool you can use to govern serving order.

Rules Governing Family Relations

Your Family can be viewed as a "team" in the business sense of the word. Many of the *rules and guidelines* for building strong teams apply equally to building a strong Family. In summary, they are:

- **Be loyal to those not present**. Family members will not discuss Family issues with Others. No personal information about Family members will be shared with Others. Parenthetically, if the slave hears someone speaking ill of another, the slave is to suggest to the complaining party that he/she find a way to discuss it directly and constructively with that person.

- **Don't complain to Others.** If the slave has a concern or complaint, it should be brought to Master. Concerns and complaints will receive a better reception if they are presented as facts/issues devoid of emotion and spin. That is, there is an "issue" and there is the "story about the issue." Master is not to be concerned with the story.

- **Do more than your fair share.** I recognize that much is required of a slave. But, that's the nature of the deal. Masters work very hard to create a mutually gratifying world both for Master and for the slave. In many cases, this is a Magical World filled with intellectual and emotional stimulation. Masters need slaves to be searching relentlessly for ways of helping support their mutual vision.

- **Be dependable.** The slave is expected to be *where* Master has indicated, *when* Master has specified, prepared to do the job-at-hand. A slave arriving late or without the proper tools is a slave who is *drifting.* You will learn how to guard against *drift* in my companion book on <u>Master/slave Relation: Handbook of Theory and Practice</u>.

- **Anticipate what Master is going to do next.** Good Family members rarely need to tell one another what to do next because the partner is already doing it. If you find that your slave is not ahead of you, able to anticipate your needs, you know that *more training* is on the horizon.

- **Be flexible.** Some people are able to act very quickly once they understand a situation. If you are one of these, then your slave must be prepared to follow quickly and without slowing you down. Your slave must learn to recognize when you are in "problem-solving" mode and learn to interject refining questions at that time – not *after* you've made a decision.

The slave's Obligations
In rank order, the slave's obligations are to his or her...

- Biological Family
- Master
- Leather Family
- Local Leather Community
- Leather Tribe

Master's Responsibilities
Master is responsible for the slave's mental, social, emotional, physical, financial and spiritual well-being. Master is responsible always

to do what is for the highest good of the slave. In the larger sense, Master will behave with respect to his slaves as, what Master Skip Chasey calls, a "Servant Master." In essence, Master will serve his slaves in ways that best help them to follow their inner Natures as they develop and mature.

> *Commentary: Being the Master in an M/s relationship involves a lot of hard work. Much of the Master's role is to support the slave's own personal growth at the same time that he trains the slave to serve him perfectly. You may want to consider putting yourself (and possibly your slave) through some work-shops and courses designed to improve your understanding of yourself and better to understand and communicate with one another. Also, taking workshops together helps to hone and develop your interpersonal skills and abilities – always a good thing.*

Concepts Specifically Relating to a slave

In Master/slave relationships, *Protocols* represent an important means to demonstrate service and obedience on a daily basis. Protocols are a way for the slave to "come present" with his or her slavery. Mastering the Protocols is something like mastering a dance form; it takes daily practice and focused concentration until the movements and processes become second nature.

Grace, Elegance and Lucidity

While a path of grace, elegance and lucidity is certainly up to you as the Master, should you seek these attributes in your slave, here is some proposed language for your protocol manual.

Master seeks to build an environment that exudes grace and ele-gance.

- The slave is responsible for identifying and employing ways of incorporating graceful movement into his or her presen-tation and style.

- The slave is expected to have and to use high-level lan-guage skills. The slave will use correct grammar and develop a vocabulary commensurate at least with that of a person entering graduate school.

- The slave is responsible for learning a pleasing vocal tonality, to modulate his/her voice, and to enunciate words clearly.

- The slave is responsible for being sensitive to personal dress and appearance at all times. In our Family, the slave is expected to be *slightly overdressed* on all public occasions.

Commentary: The concepts expressed in this section represent some of my own Core Values. I offer them to you if you feel that they resonate. They come from a viewpoint that – personally – I'm not interested in having sloppy service or sloppy people around me. When I go out in public, I'm neatly dressed; I expect my slave to be as well or better dressed than I am. As a former English teacher, I'm not interested in hearing "butchered English" from my slave.

The Concept of *Sprezzatura*

Sprezzatura is an Italian word meaning effortless technique. I first heard it at a Master/slave conference – I don't remember who was speaking. At any rate, I have adopted this concept in my own M/s relationship and I pass it on to you for your consideration. If you wish to make this concept your own, then you will communicate to your slave that he/she will view this concept as a byword, a key concept underlying all actions. You would explain that in your Household, everything is to look effortless; the house is always magically neat and tidy; clothing is always put away; meals are to come together on time and perfectly.

Commentary: True mastery is often evinced by the apparent ease with which the practitioner carries out a function or task. In my Household, I expect the slave to be so competent at tasks that others observing will not see or be distracted by the **work** *or* **effort** *involved.*

Service

In the broadest sense, the slave is always to be serving the *idea* or *concept* of the Relationship, seen through proxies such as:

- Physical appearance and bearing
- Following specified exercise routines
- Orderliness of the home and the car

Commentary: There are certain behaviors that carry beyond times when the slave is physically with you. It is going to be up to you – as stated in your own protocol manual – how you instruct your slave to look and how neat his or her car appears. If your slave lives separately from you, you get to determine how neat and clean his/her home appears. Personally, I'm not comfortable around clutter, and I grew up in a culture where the women were always coiffed and dressed – particularly to go shopping or to get on an airplane. Also, I care that my slave does not appear hurried when in public. I require a graceful gait. My slave knows how to take a seat like a lady.

Master's Expectations of the slave

Correctness in Public and Private

"A slave will always act and respond in such a way as to make the Master's orders look 'right.' A slave will never give the appearance that he thinks a Master has made a mistake, whether by facial expression, body language, or verbal challenge. Masters are not perfect, but whatever they order is 'right' because it is their will. It is the Master's will that the slave submits to, not his correctness. If the slave feels that she has information the Master is lacking, or sees a better possibility that he has not considered, the slave may – within the limits of the protocol – ask whether Master wishes her to convey such information or to make a suggestion." (Butchmann's, *Obedience and Correctness*)

If the situation involves potential or imminent peril to the life, health or safety of any individual, then the slave must act immediately and without regard to protocol. Additionally, Master may not force the slave to commit any unlawful or patently unsafe act.

In like manner, Master will refrain from publicly pointing out or making an issue of a slave's service gaffes. It is embarrassing both to the slave and to bystanders, and it can interfere with the slave's *slave-heart,* resulting in further deterioration of service. Any correction will be done in private, away from others' eyes and ears. The slave is consensually owned and thus, the slave's personal feelings must be taken into account.

> **Commentary:** *While I believe this section is quite clear, I know of an instance that occurred recently within my local Community where negotiations about establishing an M/s relationship broke down over this point. After an insensitive "correction in public," a breach of trust surfaced that even third party assistance failed to mend, despite the fact that the breach was extremely minor. The offending party couldn't/ wouldn't recognize the breach as a serious trust issue within the context of the emerging relationship.*

Reliability Builds Trust

The business world speaks of *defined repeatable processes.* In your M/s relationship, you will doubtless expect your slave to perform tasks the same way each time. After all, what else is a Protocol?

For the slave, following requests, directives or Instructions combines many positive attributes, including faithful obedience, respect, dedication and trust. While direct orders are not questioned, the slave is certainly encouraged to ask for clarification – in an effort to ensure that the job is completed correctly.

In all likelihood, you will expect your slave to exhibit the attributes of honesty, punctuality and dedication.

- **Honesty.** Being honest at all times will maximize our understanding of one another. The slave will avoid passive-aggressive behaviors, as these combine two unattractive traits: *dishonesty* and an *unwillingness to communicate directly.*

- **Dedication.** By nature, this is destined to be an intense relationship. It takes dedication and commitment to keep it going.

- **Punctuality.** Naturally, this applies to any commitment, but particularly to promptly returning phone calls and e-mail.

  o If we are meeting in town, the slave will take care to arrive early; the slave is not to keep Master waiting and will be corrected for so doing.

  o If the slave suspects that he/she will be unable to keep a time commitment, the slave must reach Master by phone to explain the delay and recommit to a revised arrival time.

Commentary: Being on time *is one of my core values. It is an expression of respect, an expression of one's personal integrity – one's ability to keep one's word. One of the very few areas that will make me angry involves the slave being late without notifying me ahead of time to revise the expected arrival time. Your protocol in this arena will depend on how YOU feel about this issue of timeliness.*

Continuing Education

Personally, I expect my slave to continue to grow emotionally and academically. Thus, my own protocol manual states that and goes on to say that from time to time, Master will enroll the slave in outside coursework meant to broaden the slave's outlook on life and/or personal skills.

Commentary: Ongoing education is another case that affects some M/s Families more than others. Knowing that I would require more from my slave than her existing level of competence, I took great care not to alarm her early in our relationship. I slowly revealed the depth and breadth of training that would be required. After three years, she has come to understand that I will enroll her in outside (commercial) training courses, seminars and classes for many, many years to come. We are a "cerebral" Family that likes to grow into new areas of interest.

Openness

"slaves exist without privacy or defenses. What they are, whatever they do, and even what they think and feel must be open for inspection at all times. slaves should always carry themselves with dignity, whether naked and in chains or out in the workaday world, and their appearance and behavior should always reflect positively on their Master and their slave brothers and sisters." (Butchmann's: *Openness*)

Availability – Cell Phone Contact

You are going to want to think through your policy about how *available* your slave is to you. For example, you might want your slave to be available 100% of the time, 24/7 by cell phone, except during such times the slave has petitioned a proposed "period of unavailability" for Master to consider. If this is so, then it needs to be in your protocol manual. If you feel that there is simply no normal time during the day or night that the slave is to be unreachable, then *that* must make it into your manual. And you will have to include specifics: "This includes times when Master and slave are out together, for instance, in different parts of the same store."

Personally, my protocol states: "The slave will keep the cell phone charged, turned on, audible and within reach at all times when not at home with Master."

> **Commentary:** *This point is important in my life. I am busy and focused. If I need to reach my slave, I need to do so NOW. I do not want to have to add a "re-contact slave" note to my list of tasks for the day. This is one of the few areas wherein I permit no latitude. To avoid becoming stressed over this point, I have instructed my slave to notify me of any periods of unavailability. Typically, this includes exercise period and before workplace meetings.*

Safewords

Your protocol manual should specify whether you are playing under SSC standards (Safe, Sane, Consensual) or under RACK standards (Risk - Aware - Consenual - Kink). For example, you could simply state: "When in Play, Master will employ RACK (rather than SSC) standards."

I also recommend that you establish an emotional safeword for your slave – particularly in a new relationship. For example, you might say: "When NOT in play, the slave will use Master's given name as an emotional safeword. That is, if the slave is in a conversation with Master and encounters an emotional landmine, using Master's given name will be interpreted by Master as a conversation-stopping event. It is interpreted as calling *RED*."

You will also need language in your manual that accounts for times when you permit your slave to play with others. Thus: "When the slave is permitted to play with other Masters, Doms or Tops, the slave is *required* to play under SSC rules, unless express permission has been granted by Master to play under RACK rules. The slave should not expect that such permission would ever be granted."

> **Commentary:** *This is not a trivial point. I agree with those within the Community who feel that the "Safe, Sane and Consensual" rules give scene-control to the bottom. After all, use of safewords in the SSC setting suggests that the bottom knows better than Master what's good for him/her. There are a number of problems with this setup. First, when a bottom goes into sub-space, it is unlikely that he or she can even call "red" – so the whole structure is defeated. Second, in Leathersex, much of the play is intended to produce catharsis. The bottom is unlikely to be able to move to that state if he/she has to monitor whether or not the play is getting too intense to be processed. Again, the SSC structure fails.*
>
> *For these reasons, we play by RACK standards: As I have said, RACK stands for "Risk-Aware Consensual Kink." Within the Community, it's assumed that you're very experienced before you will play with someone under RACK rules. Playing by RACK standards assumes that the Master knows the slave (or bottom) so well that Master can read body language and other non-verbal cues and will take the necessary actions to avoid causing harm. There are no safewords in the RACK schema. Red is just a color.*

Requests, Orders and Instructions

The slave will attend particularly to the word "Instruction." An "Instruction" is a special term in the M/s relationship. An Instruction is a Command that brooks no interference. If I am so focused on the slave doing something that I issue an Instruction, be assured that the slave is Wide Awake and taking notes. An Instruction usually carries with it a requirement to report progress to the Master. *Consequences for failure* frequently accompany an Instruction. This is not at all true for a "request" and seldom true for an "order." (Note: a "consequence" involves a "correction," not a "punishment." As I'll discuss later, *punishments* are only invoked for contract violations, not for protocol violations.)

Here are some examples of each form.

- **Request:** "Please bring me some coffee."
- **Order:** "I'd like you to be Dressed and ready to entertain our guests at 7pm tomorrow night."
- **Instruction:** "This is an Instruction: you are to keep the interior of your car as clean as it came off the showroom floor and the outside of your car is to be washed each week by Saturday noon. At no time will I enter your car if there is clutter in any of the passenger compartments."

*Commentary: I've had a love-affair with words my entire life. I am particularly attentive to the connotation of certain words. For example, one **talks to** a class or group of people and **speaks with** an individual. In my world, "talking" is rather one-sided; "speaking" is two-sided. This section sets forth distinctions that are vital in my M/s Relationship. For example, when my slave is in service to me, much of my communication involves "talking to" the slave in the sense that I am not inviting comment or conversation. On the other hand, when my slave is fulfilling "courtesan" activities, we are very much speaking with one another.*

Required to Comply

Regardless of the closeness of relations between Master and slave, the slave is admonished always to remember that a slave is a slave and, as such, subject to Master's will. In that light, the slave is required to comply with your *Contract* and with your orders and Instructions.

In my world, there is a distinction between *correction* and *punishment.*

- **Correction** is the opportunity to understand more fully the importance Master places on a Protocol or behavior. Typically, correction is administered when the slave is learning a task or a procedure and – despite a few reminders – doesn't get it right.

- **Punishment** is administered for failure to comply either with the Contract or with protocols when that failure is due to <u>willfulness</u> or <u>negligence</u> on the slave's part. Punishment is the opportunity to atone for failure. The incident that gave rise to the punishment will then be *forgiven* and not be spoken of again following the punishment debriefing. The slate is wiped clean.

Commentary #1: For example, if my slave is a passenger in the car and forgets to wait for me to come around and open the door for her, the slave should expect to be swatted on the ass. Of course, when the slave wants to be swatted, she simply opens the car door, but that's another story. At any rate, I endeavor to make "corrections" light-hearted and fun. The intention is to get the slave's attention and focus.

*Commentary #2: No action or inaction by my slave has ever arisen that required Punishment. In our three-plus years together, I've seriously invoked the "consequences clause" 4-6 times. Generally, a word about the problem or concern is sufficient. There are two reasons I don't often correct my slave. First, I recognize that my slave is very focused on being a perfect slave; and second, if my slave starts getting the idea that nothing is done **correctly**, anxiety will creep into the relationship. An anxious slave will make more mistakes, leading to* *more correction, leading to more anxiety. When this happens in a relationship, it often leads to a break up.*

In our relationship (and I also recommend this for YOUR relationship) I'm interested in catching my slave "doing right," not doing wrong. Following from that, most of my "corrections" are light-hearted. By contrast, Punishments aren't fun and certainly aren't funny.

Willful or Negligent Failure to Comply

The rare instances where the slave acts in a willful or negligent manner will result in punishment.

- No punishment will be undertaken when Master is angry.

- Before administering punishment, the slave will have the opportunity to fully explain how this Failure occurred.

- Master will ask the slave to recommend the form of Punishment.

- Master will listen to the slave's proposal and, after consideration, determine the correct course of punishment. Master will inform the slave of his decision.

- Master will use the minimum influence necessary to compel the slave's compliance with the policies and procedures the slave previously agreed to.

- Bearing in mind that Master wishes the Relationship to continue, there are no limits to the nature or extent of punishment that could be ordered as a result of the slave's act of willfulness or negligence, so long as no crime is committed (battery, death). In reality, in our relationship, *punishment* takes the path of restrictive Instructions about the use of slave's time and/or withdrawal of the slave's Time with Master.

- After punishment has been administered, Master and slave will sit down and discuss changes that may be needed in the relationship to ensure that such a breach does not occur again.

Commentary #1: An underlying assumption of the M/s dynamic is that the slave is in Internal Enslavement and will do everything possible to serve and obey to the best of his or her ability. Thus, a **willful** or **negligent** action must be taken for what it is: a cry for help by the slave. That is, the slave must be trying to get your attention through bad behavior, having failed to get your attention any other way. That's a pretty serious indictment of Master's attentiveness and mastery.

Commentary #2: In the world of BDSM M/s theory, it is generally agreed that one doesn't punish with toys used for play. That is, if you normally spank or flog or whip the slave for play, it's not appropriate to use those same instruments for punishment. On the other hand, you can purchase special floggers or whips or canes that are ONLY used for punishment. If you do this, consider purchasing a toy of totally different color or design.

Commentary #3: Personally, I believe that psychological punishment is more effective than physical punishment and this Protocol reflects my belief.

Reality Checks

With my business background, I firmly believe in "action-evaluation feedback loops." In the same way that one uses *performance reviews* for employees, I use performance reviews for my slave. I don't want any Protocol included in our lives that my slave cannot follow. [If you wish to read MUCH more about this, pick up a copy of my book: Master/slave Relations: Handbook of Theory and Practice.]

Protocol Review

These policies and procedures will be reviewed and revised periodically, as Master directs. Master will consider a request for protocol review initiated by the slave.

While the slave may suggest additions, deletions or modification to any part of this document, such suggestions should be presented for Master's consideration in written form.

Commentary: I feel strongly that every word you write down in your own Manual of Protocol is to be followed as you wrote it. If your slave is not going to follow it, you will want it removed from the Manual. If the slave would prefer to enact some protocol differently than you've described it, then you probably want to discuss this difference with your slave and decide whether you care enough about the difference either to enforce your way of doing it or to change the listed protocol to conform to the slave's preference. Personally, there have been a few occasions when my slave made recommendations that improved the efficiency of a Protocol.

I recommend that you not allow your slave to perform a sloppy imitation of a protocol. I suggest that you consider developing the attitude either that the protocol must be followed exactly or revised to conform to the way your slave seems to be able to perform it. Now, I'm not saying that your slave is dictating the protocol; I'm saying that it's easier to ride the horse in the direction it's going. That is, if your slave has trouble serving you from a Full Present position, use an Honor Present position. It's the spirit that matters, not the form.

Slave Review
Occasionally, Master will ask the slave how the slave is adapting to slavery. The slave is encouraged to use these opportunities to express concerns, fears or anxieties. If issues arise that could affect the slave's ability to serve, the slave will ask Master to schedule private time to discuss and resolve these concerns.

Chapter 2

Social Issues

Interacting with Leather Masters: Leather events

Initial meeting with a Leather Master

The slave will treat a Leather Master with the same respect and deference that the slave shows his/her Master.

The slave will **NEVER** speak to a Leather Master without specific permission or without prior introduction. When being introduced to a Leather Master, the slave will assume a submissive stance, eyes lowered.

The slave will **NOT** extend his or her hand or provide any other gesture of personal recognition. However, the slave will bow (or curtsy, if female) and remain in default position ("on point"), one pace behind and to the right of Master in a Standing Present position.

If Master decides to introduce the Dom or Master to the slave, the slave will respond to the introduction thus: "Sir, this slave is honored to meet You, Sir."

> *Commentary: This is the first time in this book that the slave has had to say something to someone other than to his/her Master.*

> **KEY COMMENTARY:** *One of the defining characteristics of the Leather Lifestyle concerns the "greeting rituals" between Leathermen and between Leathermen and submissives/slaves. When two Leathermen meet, the Leatherman of highest rank extends his hand to the Junior. Often, there is a pregnant moment while the two Leathermen try to sort out who is Senior.*

One of the most disrespectful things a slave or submissive can do when greeting a Leatherman – whether or not a Leather Master – is to smile broadly and offer a handshake. When I witness this, I'm always shaken by the split-second look of disapproval on the Leatherman's face and the quick recovery as he turns to the neophyte couple and politely asks the man: "Permission to shake your submissive's hand?" The proper response is: "Master ABC, I'd like to introduce you to my sub-missive (or slave), wxy; wxy, this is Master ABC."

Ongoing contact with a Master

The slave will follow all personal and service protocols specified in this Manual when interacting with a Master to whom the slave has been previously introduced.

> *Commentary: "Master" is a Leather title; Dom is a Not-Leather description of someone who seeks to be dominant to another. In the Introduction, I mentioned that I would address Leather protocols and Not-Leather protocols separately.*

Interacting with Doms

Relations with Doms who are not Leathermen are less formal. The slave will be courteous and respectful – but the slave will not speak to or carry on discussions with a Dom without Master's permission, unless there is an established relationship well known to Master, or unless the Dom has approached Master for such permission and that permission has been granted.

The slave does NOT have permission to ask to speak with another Dom. The Dom must first ask permission to speak with my slave.

> *Commentary: Unlike the easy social communications that can go on in the "vanilla" world (the non-kink world) with a spouse at a party or at some other social event, relations between your slave and Others involve a different frame of mind. When you think of another Master or Dom speaking with your slave, you might think of it as comparable to a person wanting to spend time with your particularly prized cat. On the one hand, you*

may be flattered that they are interested in your personal property, but on the other hand, it may strike you as a little odd that they are interested in your personal property.

Physical Proximity when Others are Present

Here are some guidelines for the slave to follow when in High Protocol and in public:

- If Master is in private discussions with a Master or Dom, the slave will remove him/herself from within earshot, but remain within eye contact. If the slave is approached by someone else during this time, the slave will inform that person that he/she is NOT free to speak, that the slave is Attending.

- The slave will not leave the position of Attending without instruction or permission to do so.

- In all other instances, the slave will maintain correct heeling position (on point).

Commentary: Although this may seem overly strict, these behaviors are necessary when other people are present so that you, as Master, can communicate at any time with your slave.

Service to Another Master, Dom or Vanilla Person

At times, the slave might have an opportunity to serve another Master or Dom. In such situations, the slave will respect their protocols and rules as best as possible, always remembering that the slave is bound by contract to **your** rules and protocols, which will at all times be respected.

If the other Master or Dom does not understand or respect the slave's existing obligations, the slave will dutifully inform them that he/she is not permitted to comply with such wishes. If there is any problem, the slave will inform Master at once in person or by phone. The slave will be VERY CAREFUL not to bring disrespect to the Family.

As Master, you need to develop a policy that governs your slave's latitude in e-mailing other people. For example, you might construct a policy something like this:

If e-mail correspondence occurs, Master is to receive a "CC" (courtesy copy – visible to the other person) so I can remain fully informed of this other relationship. When there are private meetings between my slave and another Master, Dom or vanilla man, I expect a general briefing. I will not pry into details of a relationship that I have previously approved.

> **Commentary:** Sometimes you may ask an established Master to take your slave for a period of specialized training. While the details will have been worked out between the other Master and yourself, your slave must understand that your basic rules and Instructions take precedence, and that your slave must bring Honor to your Household through his or her behavior.

Socializing in Public

Leathermen and Leatherwomen (Leatherfolk) are often referred to as a *Tribe*. The slave's relations with Tribe members will be different from the slave's relations with Doms from the Not-Leather BDSM community.

This section contains some suggested language for protocols governing pubic appearances.

Relations in a Leather Setting
Leatherfolk will understand our Protocols and Symbols and will respect my slave's position within our Family. Similarly, my slave will recognize and respect protocols and symbols of Leathermen from other Families. Under NO CIRCUMSTANCES will this slave touch a Leatherman without specific permission. This is a serious sign of *disrespect* and will result in Correction.

In the presence of Leatherfolk, Masters shall be awarded the respect of their positions. The slave will refer to them by the honorific by which they are introduced, and afforded the courtesy given to Master.

subs will be acknowledged as such and the slave may converse casually with them *in the appropriate setting* once permission has been granted. **It is NOT appropriate to converse casually with a submissive or another slave while in active service to Master or if a scene is taking place.**

In the event that a Leatherman endeavors to hug my slave, but this person *has not negotiated with me* for permission, the slave will accept the hug – *but not return the hug* – with grace and tact, careful to avoid publicly embarrassing this person. If this situation occurs out of Master's sight, or occurs a second time, the slave will inform the novice Leatherman that he/she is in Protocol and, with respect, does not have permission to return the hug. The slave will stand still during this exchange, but then leave the area promptly to report the incident.

> *Commentary: This issue comes up occasionally in Austin because we're a "huggy" community. No offense is intended. Leatherfolk will ask: "Permission to hug?" before offering the hug, and a slave's Master will "give the nod." However, the protocols in this section govern the behavior you might expect from your slave when in a more formal Leather setting.*

Use of Furniture

In our home, in private, the slave is permitted to use furniture, unless directed not to.

When attending an event in High Protocol the slave will not use furniture, unless specifically directed to do so. If the use of furniture is necessary for some medical reason, the slave will inform me in private, preferably before the situation presents itself.

> *Commentary: Use/non-use of furniture is more of an issue in the Not-Leather community than in the world of Leather. Nonetheless, it is a powerful indicator of relative status. But, at this writing I'm 61 and my slave is 50, so requiring my slave to sit on the floor in the privacy of our living room strikes me as more severe than necessary. The slave knows that she is my property whether she is curled up at my feet or sitting next to me. And, if there is some question about that, shame on me.*

Relations in a Not-Leather BDSM Setting
Hugging: The slave is free to hug any other submissive, *if and only if,* the slave has asked Master to negotiate with that submissive's Dom either for initial or for ongoing permission to hug this Dom's submissive.

The slave is free to accept a hug from any Dom whom the slave KNOWS has negotiated that ongoing permission with me. In other cases, the slave will inform the Dom endeavoring to offer a hug that he (the Dom) must first obtain such permission from Master.

Speaking: If Master indicates that you are in High Protocol, the slave may not converse in public. If someone approaches the slave, the slave will lower his/her eyes and say: "Sir/Ma'am: this slave is in High Protocol tonight and may not speak."

> *Commentary: Once again, these speaking, greeting and hugging protocols communicate the M/s dynamic within the BDSM environment. Such protocols keep the relationship up-front both in the Master's and in the slave's minds – and broadcasts it to those nearby. Interestingly, this is also a way to share the celebration of one another with other Leatherfolk.*

Special Situations

Being Loaned Out Overnight
In rare instances, the slave may be loaned out to another Dom or Master to learn a skill or for some practical service. Special rules govern the slave at these times.

- All activity expected of the slave will be pre-negotiated between Master and the person to whom the slave is being loaned (hereinafter: Host).

- Master will know the physical location where the slave is or will be. This assumes that the slave has been loaned to someone well-known to Master. If the person is *not well-known*, then standard safe-call rules apply. (See Appendix B for discussion of the safe-call process.)

- If sexual intercourse is involved, this MUST be pre-negotiated with Master and condoms must be used.

- For other play, the slave must not be marked.

The slave will phone Master upon arrival at the destination and will telephone Master at precisely 9 A.M. while on loan.

If the slave is spending multiple days/nights on loan, the slave will also check in with Master precisely at noon and in the evening before 9 P.M. (at the convenience of the slave's Host). [Intent: not to require the slave to make an evening phone call that might interrupt the flow of evening activities.]

When speaking with Master in these situations, the slave will use the following communications code:

1. Emergency and call the police;

2. Emergency, come get me as soon as you can;

3   Not an emergency, but I don't feel comfortable. Please ask the Host to release me now. I can get home on my own;

4   No problem but not a very interesting experience – I'll stick it out;

5   Good experience, I'm having a nice time and hope to be loaned out to this person again, if it Pleases Master.

Commentary: Readers familiar with the use of "safe-calls" will immediately realize that some form of coded message must be used. For any readers not familiar with safe-calls, the issue is that if the person is being held against his or her will and threatened, you cannot simply ask: "Hey, howyadoen out there? Feelin safe?" With a gun to his/her head, the answer will always be: "Oh, sure. No problem, I'm just fine. He's a great guy. No need for me to call you again."

So, when you receive the check-in call, I suggest that you open with: "Good morning, what's the Code number?" You probably don't want to start "chatting" until you have the number. This way, if it's a "one" you don't need to hear any more and the slave had the opportunity to get it out.

*I take this coded message system **extremely seriously** and my slave and I always review it carefully before the slave is released to go to the rendezvous.*

Reminders

The slave will write a formal "thank you" note to the Host within 24 hours after the visit. As usual, Master will be "copied" on all e-mails.

The slave does not have *prima facie* permission to maintain contact with the Host, either telephonic or e-mail. Permission for the Host to speak or write to the slave must be sought by the Host from Master. If the Host contacts the slave without Master's prior permission, the slave will explain to that Host that he/she must ask Master for permission to speak with or to write to the slave.

Relations with Family and Friends

You will probably want your slave to maintain family relationships. One way to handle that is as follows:

> The slave will maintain family relationships and will inform Master if an order in some way limits that family contact. The slave will keep Master apprised of family-related scheduling issues.

Particularly in this political climate, it is imperative that minor children be insulated from any kinky activities or unusual relationship issues. Some language about that could be:

> Minor children should not be made aware of the slave's status. Uninvolved adults should not be made fully aware of the slave's status. The slave is encouraged to maintain friendships with people who are aware of, and generally approve of, our lifestyle.

> ***Commentary:*** *Have you noticed that when you enthusiastically describe your M/s relationship with your slave to someone outside our Community, you get the sense that you shouldn't*

have said anything? I counsel saying as little as possible to anyone. Those who are not in the lifestyle simply don't have enough knowledge to be able to appreciate how special the M/s dynamic is.

Outside Friendships

As Master, you are responsible for your slave's social wellbeing. You will want to consider protocols that address that issue. Here are some examples:

The slave is specifically encouraged to develop and maintain friendships with others, whether male, female, Dom, slave or submissive. The slave will advise Master when opportunities are available to interact with others, so that time for this activity can be allotted, if possible.

Occasionally, the slave may ask to host friends for an in-house function. If allowed, the slave may host the event, taking care to protect our property and privacy. The slave is responsible for the conduct of guests and for returning the house to an orderly state.

The slave may be permitted to spend time with acquaintances for dinners, movie outings, camping, etc. At Master's pleasure, these occasions may range from hours to several days in duration. The slave remains "on duty" during these occasions, remaining in full compliance with our contract and all protocols pertaining to personal behavior, dress and activities.

Commentary: Once again, the slave is valuable property. Master has invested a great deal of time, trouble and expense in training this slave. Master is always concerned with the quality and quantity of experiences to which the slave is exposed. The slave is always to be sensitive to the unusual nature of the personal relationship with Master. These protocols reinforce that difference.

Chapter 3

Seamless Integration of Concept to Action

As a Master of your own slave, you are solely responsible for tailoring every suggested protocol to suit your own particular situation and preference. Here, I've endeavored to put down a wide range of topics and suggested protocols for your consideration.

Standing Orders

Chain of Command
The slave serves Master. *Serving Master* is the slave's sole purpose.

Levels of Protocol
We will use no level of protocol around minors. For all other times there are three levels of protocol; each builds upon the other:

- **Social Protocol.** The slave refers to Master as "Master" or "Sir," but has no other language restriction. The slave is free to speak and to ask questions without limitation. The slave may walk *almost* next to Master and in all other ways appear to be part of a "vanilla" couple. In a group setting, the slave is released from having to maintain eye contact at all times.

- **Low Protocol.** Low Protocol is used when out in public (as in a mall or at a restaurant). Walking and standing protocols are invoked. The slave will not sit until Master has been seated. The slave will remain in eye contact with Master and will ask permission to go somewhere out of eyesight. However, the slave will not be required to stand "on point" (described later).

- **High Protocol.** All formal protocols are invoked – most especially the *languaging* and *attending* protocols. The slave's sole purpose is to serve Master and to make Master's life easier; the slave is *not* free to engage in discourse. The slave is expected to remain *highly alert* to any logistical issue or problem that may need to be solved (such as reminding Master of someone's name or taking a business card being offered to Master from another person). The slave will remain "on point" at all times, shadowing Master's every move.

Commentary: Because formal Protocols can be tricky and require practice, I use them every time my slave and I are together for dinner. That is, for the period up to dinner, we are either in low or in social protocol. But, once we've showered and dressed for dinner (more on this, later) we conduct our "recommitment" ceremony and from that point until we go to bed, we're in High Leather Protocol.

Accessibility

The slave will be accessible by phone at all times. The slave will leave the cell phone turned on at ALL TIMES, including while charging. The slave is to be sure the cell phone is within hearing even in the slave's own home and is to carry the cell phone even when Master and the slave are out together, as previously referenced.

Any change in this arrangement, even for a few minutes, requires Permission.

Commentary: The "cell phone issue" is another example that may appear overly strict. This may be more MY issue than it is YOUR issue. I can only say that this protocol has been worded this way to fit the way I am and the way I require my slave to be.

Agreements

For *things that matter*, Master operates in the world of structured Agreements. Agreements have four components:

- State the offer/acceptance; (I agree...).
- Specify the general item to be done; (...to wash the outside of the car...).
- List conditions of satisfaction – be clear about the level of activity   (...so that all the dirt and tar are completely removed and no water spots remain...).
- Specify the time frame (...within the next two hours.).

If the slave suspects that it will not be possible to fully accomplish any of the four aspects of the Agreement, the slave is cautioned NOT to enter into the agreement – this is the time to explain the conflict/issue; this is a time for honesty and integrity. The modification of any aspect of an Agreement *must* be done BEFORE the agreement is accepted, or as soon as the need for modification becomes apparent.

If the slave has made an Agreement and something comes up that makes it impossible to fulfill the Agreement on time or in the way agreed upon, the slave will contact Master and discuss the situation before the time period expires.

Failure to keep an Agreement will carry Consequences.

Commentary: In my world, Agreements are a big deal. I don't use them casually. I don't mind modifying an agreement on the front end. I don't even mind being contacted regarding a change to the deadline. However, I mind a great deal if no effort was made to renegotiate the terms and conditions of an Agreement and it is not fulfilled exactly as it was set. Most of the train-wrecks that occur between my slave and me concern the slave's failure to keep me informed that the content of an Agreement has changed or that the time period for completion has changed.

Because I am so focused on keeping Agreements perfectly, I caution my slave not to enter lightly into a formal Agreement with me. I'm going to be easier to get along with if the slave says: "Master, I cannot fulfill the terms you are proposing," rather than entering into the Agreement suspecting that the terms cannot be fulfilled.

I will comment further on this point. I've known people who would agree to do about anything with little or no intention of doing so. In my doctoral year, I had a professor who would promise anything just to get you to go away. While at first everyone in the program thought that he was being coopera-tive and helpful, he was simply manipulative. His behavior was passive-aggressive. Aware of my personal sensitivity to this point – that I will aggressively challenge any failure to keep an Agreement – I explain it to those who work closely with me. Similarly, on those occasions that I feel an Agreement is needed to accomplish some significant Task, I'm careful to review the component parts of an Agreement and remind the slave of the importance of communicating changes to me **ahead of time**.

Time Commitments

While it may not be so in YOUR Household, in my own Household issues of *time* are important. *Time commitments* represent a daily opportunity to keep your word. They are a form of Agreement.

If the slave has been told an arrival or departure time, Master expects that time to be honored with precision. There will be Consequences to violating time issues.

Commentary: "Keeping one's word" is a core concept within the Leather culture. From the very beginning of my exposure to the Leather World, I was struck by the degree of honesty, integrity and high moral purpose I found there. If a Leatherman says something will be done, you can be sure it will be. If I, as Master, have told someone that I will arrive at a certain time, tardiness by my slave will NOT cause me to be late to that meeting. Although this has never happened, if my slave were not to be ready to leave on time, I would leave and let my slave consider the Consequences.

Health and Hygiene
Master may permanently mark or modify the slave's body to suit our purposes.

- The slave's body will be maintained in a manner that ensures good health and provides for our sexual enjoyment. Specifically, the slave will keep weight reasonably proportional to height and build. Pursuant to that, the slave will exercise according to specific Instructions provided at Master's pleasure.

- The slave will attempt to avoid disease. Should medical or dental attention be required, the slave will advise Master and promptly seek appropriate care. The slave will have annual physical, dental and other appropriate exams.

- The slave's pubic area will be shaved daily.

Commentary: This section is pretty straightforward. As the Master is responsible for the slave's physical well being, topics in this section are really pro forma. Said differently, Master is ensuring that his property remains in good, clean working order to be of maximum use and availability. I do not require anything of my slave that I do not exact upon myself. I exercise, seek medical attention promptly, shave daily, etc.

Issues of Communication
Courtesies and conversations often rely on *tact*. *Tact* is the talent for not saying that you were right in the first place. In our Family, we are not interested in affixing *blame;* we are interested in developing rich, harmonious relationships. The relevant aphorism is: "we're not put on this earth to see through one another, but to see one another through."

Silent Hand Signals
When in public, there will be times when you need to communicate with the slave. If alone, it's easy enough simply to tell the slave what you wish; however, if others are around or if you are in a Leather setting, it is often more pleasing to communicate silently to the slave. To avoid confusion, I recommend only a few silent signals.

STOP or SILENCE: If walking, fold the right arm up to shoulder height, close to the body and display a closed fist; the slave knows to stop immediately (as opposed to running into you). Use the same signal if already stopped (or sitting) and you wish the slave either to stop speaking or not to start speaking.

COME TO ME or I want to say something to you: When entertaining Others or when out in public (whether or not it is a Leather event), the slave always keeps Master in view. By placing the first and second fingers of your hand on your opposite bicep, the slave knows immediately to Attend you.

Commentary #1: Much of the mystery and magic that accompanies an M/s couple in public concerns their dance, the effortless way they move together. Part of the magic is created through the use of silent gestures. Here, I've only touched on two basic gestures; I'll describe more when we get to the section about how to present. For some people a "scene" consists of whips or floggers; for others, a scene is created through protocols – every time you are together.

Commentary #2: Let's look closely at the silent signal for Come to Me. Whether you use your right hand fingers on your left bicep or your left hand fingers on your right bicep may or may not have any significance in your world. On the other hand, if you are heavily into symbolism, then it may make most sense to use fingers from your left hand (dominant side) placed on your right bicep (submissive side).

Conversation Conventions in this Family

In our Family, there are three overriding principles when non-Family members are present. You may wish to consider adapting them to your world.

- First: don't correct a Family member in public. All corrections are conducted in private. Violation of this Protocol will have dramatic consequences, because it communicates disharmony and lack of respect.

- Second: "It's better to be interested than interesting." Don't go on at length about how much you know about some topic or where you've been in the world.

- Third: Humility is a good thing. We all have plenty to be humble about.

Commentary: In conversations, we make a point of supporting people, not demonstrating how clever we can be. No one likes to be "outshone" in public; no one likes to be corrected in public. Such actions display personal insecurity as well as discourtesy towards others. Worse, if directed towards a Family member, it risks displaying disunity within the Family. Apart from all that, it undermines relationships and demonstrates poor manners.

Direct Questions from Another
When the slave doesn't know the answer to a direct question...:

- Admit it. No one is expected to know everything. The slave will gain more "points" for admitting they don't know something than in trying to concoct or guess at the answer.

- Find out the answer and tell the person. The form of response, here, is: "Sir, I don't know the answer, but I will find out and tell you, Sir."

- The slave must complete this "loop" and get the answer promptly to the promised person; the slave must live in Integrity.

When the slave DOES know the answer to a direct question, *but the slave fears that the person asking the question won't like the answer,* consider the following:

- First, is this "small talk" to keep the conversation going, or is it a serious "content" discussion? If small talk, providing a refined or more accurate correction might kill the mood. If it is a serious discussion and the speaker is not being precise or accurate, the slave will have to weigh the consequences of "being right" by providing better information.

- For our Family purposes, my preferred "transition phrase" in this kind of situation is: "It seems to me I read somewhere…" – then give the correct answer. This leaves open the possibility that the slave may not be remembering the fact exactly. It softens the blow.

*Commentary: While people are generally driven to please and to give answers that please, my experience is that one gains more "personal points" for admitting they **don't know something** and providing the answer later, if at all. In like manner, I have found that there are **often** times when it's FAR BETTER to avoid providing better or more complete explanations about a discussion topic, as the less informed person dislikes being shown up in public.*

Jokes: This is a touchy subject for me. You may not share my own sensitivity to certain categories of humor. At any rate, here is a protocol to consider:

The slave will be wary of jokes. Master is VERY sensitive about jokes. In our Family, there will be **NO** jokes where a person or sub-culture is the subject or where a person's condition (being Polish, Jewish, blonde, poor, dumb…) is ridiculed. Personal stories are not considered to be jokes.

Taboo Subjects: The well-known three: religion, race and politics plus topics such as: death, disasters, accidents, serious illness and – with Elders present – their age or mine. (I don't appreciate phrases such as: "Oh, he's a much older man – about **your** age.")

Conversational Ease
Everyone associated with this Family is expected to speak grammatically correct English and to strive to build a large and rich vocabulary.

To be a good conversationalist, one must first have something to say. Second, one must be able to say it well. To achieve the first goal – having something to say – members of this Family are expected to have personal areas of competence and maintain at least a passing familiarity with current events. Poor grammar and/or the use of a simple vocabulary seriously inhibit one's ability to communicate effectively. Words communicate concepts. An advanced vocabulary improves one's ability to communicate and understand complex ideas.

Commentary: These Protocols fit my background and preferences. They may not fit yours. I spend a great deal of my time around highly educated people. They are susceptible to judging negatively people with poor grammar and simple vocabulary. While I certainly don't want my slave to behave pretentiously, it is important to me that my slave speaks grammatically correct English with accuracy and lucidity.

It is almost equally important that my slave can demonstrate our interest in other people's ideas by asking intelligent, thought-provoking questions that draw others into discourse. My slave's grammar and vocabulary should contribute to the conversation, demonstrating our high regard for those whose company we enjoy, rather than distracting from it by jarring the senses (like discordant music).

When our company feels flattered by our interest, it builds camaraderie, encourages people to include us in further rich and stimulating discussion. When my slave can contribute interesting questions to a conversation, not only can it benefit me by broadening my experience, but also can minimize the discomfort I sometimes feel when conversations are reduced to banalities and small talk.

In our personal case, my slave and I frequently exercise our "vocabulary kink" in the evenings by poring over the Oxford English Dictionary, *happily chasing down one rabbit trail after another in this fifteen-volume set of dictionaries that weigh about seven pounds each. At this writing, we are reading the* Dictionary of Differences *(Parragon Books, 1993) during our evening meal. Here, we explore and discuss differences between such words as: poring/pouring, decry/descry and tortuous/torturous.*

Honesty in Verbal Communication

Here is another in a string of *core values* for you to consider when designing your own protocols. In this first case, I start with an *assertion,* then go on to describe the related protocol.

It is critical that all Family Members be honest and direct in all their dealings. One can avoid a great deal of embarrassment by giving precise answers to questions asked by Seniors (the term used in the Leather Community for a Leatherman more experienced than the person to whom the Senior is addressing). If the slave cannot give a complete or correct answer, then answer only as much of the question as possible without being misleading or evasive. It is always appropriate to say: "Sir, this slave doesn't know, Sir (or Ma'am), but i will find out and let you know." If the slave offers this response, be sure to write a note that the slave now owes this person an answer. When the slave takes on an obligation of this sort, it would be well to inform Master of the exchange *in writing.*

> *Commentary: The last sentence is Very Important. The slave has taken on an Obligation as Master's representative, but at this point it is an Obligation **not specifically assigned by Master**. Thus, the slave **must** inform Master about it – really quickly and thoroughly. Failure to do so is willful and against the spirit of the M/s dynamic. Because I tend to forget easily, I write notes about practically everything. If the slave gives me a **note**, I can easily file it electronically, so that I keep track of my slave's obligation. If the slave **tells me** of some idea, plan or future action, I am likely to forget that the conversation ever took place.*

Rank and Respect

While the Senior may rarely think of it when speaking with a junior (again, the term used in the Leather Community for the less senior Leatherperson), the junior will never forget their difference in rank. This is as it should be. Understanding this maxim should make it easy to speak respectfully with those of different standing within our Community; violation may bring embarrassment.

Courtesies to Juniors

Those associated with our Family will exhibit the utmost courtesy and caring aid to juniors, particularly juniors who are being mentored; they will be made to feel welcomed and honored. Any discourtesy towards others reflects poorly on the Honor and Integrity of the Family and will be viewed in that light.

Conflict in Conversations

The occasion may arise when someone states an opinion that substantially opposes the slave's opinion. Unless some action is called for on the slave's part, the slave is to ignore the comment out of respect for the Senior's greater age or experience. If the slave is asked for his/her specific opinion on this matter and cannot avoid answering, the form of reply is: "With due respect, Sir, in this matter of opinion my experience has been to the contrary." The slave may then express the contrary opinion based on experience.

> **Commentary:** *In our Family, I strongly discourage countering a* **non-fact-based opinion** *with another non-fact-based opinion. That is, if a Family member doesn't know the answer, we don't guess.*

Apologies for Social Gaffes

If the slave has harmed or hurt someone needlessly or through carelessness, the slave must do more than apologize; the slave must ask this person's forgiveness. If the slave fails to keep an appointment, he/she must telephone, e-mail or write a brief note explaining the failure to do so – and the reason must be a good one.

In a High Protocol setting, if the slave is asked by a Dom or Master to carry out some non-trivial request, the proper response is: "Sir, that question must be asked of Master; this slave does not have the authority to grant you such a request."

If the slave breaks or damages something, the slave will try to replace the article exactly. If this is not possible, the slave will then send flowers or a book of interest to the person with a note apologizing for the mishap.

In a non-Leather setting, if the slave steps or passes in front of someone, or bumps into them, the slave will say: "Please excuse me" or "I beg your pardon." In High Protocol, the slave will say: "Sir, please excuse this slave's clumsiness" or "This slave apologizes for having bumped you, Sir."

> **Language Commentary:** I presume that you, the reader, caught the shift in personal reference between the "vanilla" and "Leather" settings. The slave said: "excuse **me**" in the vanilla setting – indicating an awareness of self. In the Leather setting, the slave referred to him/herself in the passive voice: "Please excuse this slave's...". The degree to which you, as Master, permit your slave to express a personal awareness of self is your decision. For an extensive exploration of the concept of objectification in the M/s relationship, see SlaveMaster's outstanding website: www.bornslaves.com.

> **Overall Commentary:** Again, the slave represents Master, and your Family's "social IQ" will be transmitted through the slave's social circle like wildfire, whether in a "vanilla" or "Leather" setting. Nothing should be asked of the slave that you would not do yourself.

Behavior in Public

This set of protocols establishes a *way of being* in the world both for the Master and the slave. These protocols help to affirm Master's expectation that the slave will always be available and attentive when they are together. Because the slave walks with Master, shadowing his/her footsteps, some rules have to be established about how this "shadow-person" moves and behaves. If the slave is to *serve* Master and *not to be a burden* to Master, the slave must know how to keep out of the way and how to be helpful.

These sample protocols are designed to be taken as-is or adapted to your particular M/s structure.

Standing
Any time the slave is in public with Master, the slave will assume the "on point" position. That is, the slave will maintain Public Present position ("parade rest") slightly behind Master's right shoulder. So long as Master is standing, the slave will remain standing in that physical location. If Master wishes the slave to come around to a position facing him, he will either instruct the slave to move into his range of vision or use the Family's silent hand signal to cause the slave to change positions (two fingers of the left hand on the right bicep).

If the slave is seated on a chair or on the floor, the slave will stand whenever Master enters or leaves the same room or space – unless Master waives this protocol by an immediate order to "sit," "stay," or "continue."

Sitting
It is my wish that the slave sit on furniture unless High Protocol is invoked, in which case the slave will not sit on any furniture without a direct and specific order by Master. However, if we are in a "kinky" setting (lecture, etc) and there are insufficient chairs for all the Doms or Masters, my slave is to curl up at my feet.

Walking
The slave normally walks in a position that I refer to as "on point." That is, to the right and about one step behind Master. The slave is to assume a position that is natural, yet reflects our respective rank. The slave is to be near enough so that Master can be heard when giving orders. In "Vanilla" settings, the slave's hands may be at his/her side. However, in High Protocol, the slave will walk with hands in the "parade rest" position.

Eating
For egregious detail, the slave is referred to the chapter discussing *dining rituals*. In summary, the protocols are as follows:

- Master will seat the slave at the table; under no circumstances will the slave take a seat unless Master has directed this action.

- Once seated, the slave will sit motionless until Master completes the "centering" ceremony. Note: if we are eating in a restaurant and sitting in a booth rather than in chairs, this step is omitted. [Note: You will have to make up a *centering ceremony* of your own – or omit this step. It is simply a brief ceremony that celebrates that we are eating a meal together and appreciate being alive.]

- Once Master is seated, the slave will wait until Master removes his napkin and places it on his/her lap before doing the same. The slave will take care to unfold the napkin so that it remains half-folded; when placed in the lap, the crease faces toward the body.

- If this is an evening meal with cocktails or wine, the slave will wait until Master has offered the first toast before sipping.

- The slave will not eat a morsel of food from any course of the meal until Master has first taken a bite and then fed a single bite to the slave, who will proceed to eat at a pace set by Master. When Master places fork and knife across his plate to signal that he has finished eating, the slave will do the same regardless of any food left on the slave's plate.

- The slave will closely monitor all beverages Master is drinking and ensure that they are kept filled without prompting.

Commentary: These protocols are designed to bring ceremony into everyday life. Personally, I wish to celebrate as many aspects of Life as possible, to recognize even the ordinary and commonplace aspects as special. Dining offers many opportunities to do so.

Doors and Elevators

The slave will open doors and elevators (and any related apparatus), then stand aside for Master to pass through; the slave follows. In the case of elevators, the slave will enter after all others and then press the elevator buttons for Master, as needed. The slave will remain in the elevator, holding the door until Master has exited.

In the case of door configurations where there is an outer and inner door, the slave will open the first door to let Master pass, then enter and – as Master waits – open the second door.

Should Master be walking with another Dom or Master, Master will open the second door to let the guest enter, then turn the second door over to the slave to hold while Master enters. The slave will then follow behind.

Should a third person be present with us, we discuss door protocols beforehand; but, the general concept is that the slave is Master's *Personal Assistant* and must remain "attached" to Master at all times. Thus, if the slave is holding a door, the slave will enter after Master and turn any remaining "door holding" duties over to the third.

> *Commentary: This may sound complicated, but it is not. These protocols are relevant because we are sometimes out with a "Third" who is not a slave and does not participate in these Protocols. In those times, it is logical for my slave to enter after me and let this Third follow behind. Because my slave does not serve this Third, it would not make sense for my slave to hold a door for him/her.*

> *When the Third is part of the Leather Lifestyle and acts as the junior slave when with us, she/he will be expected to move ahead of my slave to open and hold a door or elevator until both my slave and I have passed through.*

Driving
There are times when the slave will serve Master as *chauffeur* (discussed later). In those instances, the slave will open the door for Master to enter and to exit the passenger side of the car. If Master is driving, Master will open the passenger side door for the slave.

> *Commentary: As our M/s dynamic has evolved, my slave often serves as my chauffeur. As you will read later, when fulfilling this role the slave is dressed entirely in black (including black blazer) and wears a chauffeur's cap. (I'm a little eccentric.)*

Handshakes
Leather Protocol calls for personal reserve; under no circumstances will this slave extend a hand to a Dom unless the slave knows that such a gesture has been pre-negotiated and approved.

If the slave DOES have permission to shake hands or to hug another Dom/Master, this slave will attend to the length of such contact. Contact must be socially appropriate in order not to be misinterpreted as a "forward" gesture.

When a submissive in our Family shakes hands with (or hugs) another submissive, the less senior, or if this is unknown, the *younger or less experienced submissive,* waits for the older or higher ranking submissive to extend his/her hand in greeting. Junior submissives *rise* to greet more senior submissives. In Low Protocol and Social Protocol settings, the slave is to follow polite gestures of hospitality.

> *Commentary:* The action of a slave or submissive extending a hand to a Dom or Leatherman in a Leather setting is a HUGE breach of protocol within the community.

Introductions
The less senior Leatherman is always presented to the more senior Leatherman. "Master Steve, may I present George?"

Even in settings that are not Leather, avoid automatically introducing a Dom to another Dom's submissive. When such introduction is required, the Host Dom will ask the Dom responsible for the submissive to make the introduction, thus: "George, may I ask you to present boy william to your submissive?"

When making a presentation, the name of the higher ranked Dom is always spoken first.

> *Commentary:* There are regional differences in protocols used within the BDSM community in the US. I can only write from my experience that there is no particular expectation that a Dom who is not in a Leather setting will feel the slightest inclination to introduce his submissive to another Dom. In Leather

settings, there is more formality and more formal courtesy (and less perceived threat of competition); Masters frequently always introduce their slaves when in social settings.

Forms of Address

After reviewing many examples of speech protocols, I adopted those set forth on the Butchmann's Academy website. I recommend them for your consideration. They are written in the first person, so you can get feel the way the protocol would be written.

My slave(s) will address me as "Master" or "Sir" in every sentence uttered (e.g.: "Master, permission to leave the room?"). Others who are associated with the Family in submissive positions, but *not* as slaves, will address me as "Sir." Those associated with the Family will address other Doms or Masters as "Sir", unless the individual is a recognized Leather Master, in which case the honorific "Master" will be used along with the person's name (e.g.: Master Skip or Master Steve).

Until formally introduced, my slave has no reason to speak to any Master, Leatherman or Dom. Thus, the slave should already know whether or not the person is a Leather Master.

Speaking in Public – Social or Leather Event

If the slave has something to communicate to Master, the slave will move into Master's range of vision and **wait to be recognized.** The slave is **not** to speak until recognized, unless responding to Master's questions or until the slave has been invited to participate in an ongoing conversation. Once a conversation is started, the slave is free to speak until that conversation ends, at which point the process repeats.

Commentary: This is another example of the kind of protocol that can vary between Owners. For example, the strict view is that willfully speaking in public is not permitted. A different Owner may wish his or her slave to behave differently on this point. Also, you may wish to work out a code so that your slave can signal you when there is something important to say on occasions when you would normally prefer the slave's silence.

Serving

When serving food or drinks, the slave will follow the previously discussed concept of *sprezzatura* (effortless technique). The relevant protocols are:

- Approach slowly and with grace. DO NOT APPEAR HURRIED or harrowed.

- Hold a plate with both hands underneath.

- Hold a long stemmed wine glass with base resting on left hand and with right hand stabilizing the stem of the glass.

- Hold a coffee mug or glass of liquid (**filled only ¾ full**) by placing it directly on the slave's left or right hand, half of the mug on the fingers, half on the palm of the hand, the other hand holding up the hand that holds the mug. The slave is forbidden to stabilize the coffee mug in any other way.

- Hold a cup and saucer in the same fashion.

- Should any liquid be spilled, the slave is to remove the food/liquid, clean the spill and start over from the beginning.

- Before handing Master the food/beverage, the slave will assume a "full present" position and, with deliberation, kiss the edge of the plate/glass/mug/cup with eyes lowered. The slave will then look up into Master's eyes and present the gift with a slow and deliberate gesture. Note: the *intent*, here, is that the slave **focus** attention on the moment; that the slave demonstrate cognizance of his/her status and the importance of the ceremony of *service*.

- The slave will then rise to a standing position by rolling backward in one single, fluid motion; the slave will not use either foot for stability. That is, the slave will roll back from a kneeling position to a squatting position with both knees together and then use both legs to rise to a standing position. There will be no "jerkiness" in this action. (Note 1: the secret is to use the weight of the head to provide stability. Note 2: women in heels may have some trouble with this and be better off serving from an Honor Present position, rather than a Full Present position.)

• The slave will then stand for the count of three (demonstrating *intentionality*), bow/curtsy and take three small steps backward, turn and leave. Note: the slave will **not** turn their back on Master prior to taking three backward steps.

*Commentary: This Protocol is about being present during serving rituals. As service is one of the core concepts of M/s relations; **how** that service is rendered becomes an Issue. I am* extremely *"present" with my slave. I pay attention to every move and revel in its perfection. I would never ignore my slave's efforts by not being mentally and emotionally present.*

Communication

Timely and Relevant
The slave will contact me in a timely manner by phone and/or e-mail to express needs or to report on anything relevant to my life. I prefer not to be told of events or issues that are not germane to our relationship; if possible, the slave should "manage" or "handle" such situations without involving me.

Commentary: Life is complicated and busy enough without the slave adding to it with unrelated issues/concerns. The slave's role is to remove problems from my life, not to add problems. Since small issues can grow larger if not caught early, timeliness in communication is important.

Expressing Dissatisfaction
Pre-topic commentary: This section discusses the slave's **attitude**. Let's be real about this: chances are that your slave is a vibrant person with profound feelings. For your relationship to work, it must be fulfilling for both parties. If the slave is unhappy, Master will be unhappy (and probably pretty quickly). It's important that the slave communicate appropriately any unhappiness at receiving an Order or Instruction.

Should the slave feel the need to express hurt feelings or the sense of being overtaxed in some way, the slave is instructed to communicate these sentiments in an appropriate manner as soon as they are recognized.

- "Appropriate manner" can be: "Master, with respect, I'm feeling overburdened with this task. May I explain my current workload?"

- "Master, **when you**... **I feel**... **because**..." (Note: this is my preferred formula for communicating an emotional issue.)

Commentary: In my view, most interpersonal issues and problems arise among couples – whether in Vanilla or BDSM relationships – because the couple (usually the man) lacks the skills to maneuver around and through emotional upsets. This is a case where the more counseling/therapy and study the Master has put into learning how to understand and work with Others, the better the chance that the M/s relationship will survive. I know a number of men who have tried M/s relationships over and over and over and they just can't quite figure out why they don't work. The answer, in my opinion, is that these Doms lack the interpersonal skills to build solid, nurturing, long-term relationships whether in the "vanilla" or the kink world.

In my view, it all rests in each member of the M/s couple being willing to admit that they can be wrong, usually about an emotional issue.

Apologies

"Sir, this slave begs your pardon, Sir" is how the slave expresses regret for an accidental mishap. You probably don't want your slave to say, "I'm sorry", or "Excuse me," as these forms imply that the slave acted willfully (use of "I" or "me") – that may be contrary to the way you are training your slave.

The more you study M/s relations and the more you work with a slave, the more you understand the importance of getting the slave to understand thoroughly that a slave has no free will; that the slave is serving YOUR will exclusively. The rare times that my slave gets into trouble with me usually involves her having taken a personal initiative during a time when the slave had been given a time-sensitive task. That is: after specific discussions, I understood that my slave was going to do "X" over the lunch hour and the next thing I know I'm confronted either with my slave having done "Y" and not "X," or with my slave having done "X" plus "Y" without re-negotiating the deal. This is seriously "not-OK" with me and leads to immediate Consequences.

Oral Communications

I wish my slave to use the words "Master" or "Sir" in every sentence. My *request* is that this protocol is always followed, regardless of the social setting or stated protocol level.

Written Communications

The Protocol for written communications to Master is as follows:

- Opens the communication with "Master;"
- Capitalizes the first letter in any reference to me (e.g.: "You, Your" etc.);
- Uses lowercase in any reference to him/herself (e.g.: "i");
- Mixes upper/lowercase in references to both of us (e.g.: use "U/us" not "us"); and
- Closes with a lowercase name in the last sentence.

Commentary: I'm not sure whether or not these writing protocols come from the world of Leather or from the het world or from the Internet. I've seen them used in all three situations. At any rate, I have adopted them as protocols I wish my slave to use, but that's my personal decision.

E-mail Communications with Others

The slave will copy Master when writing to ANY Dom/Domme or Leatherman. The slave must have permission to initiate and/or to maintain such communication.

Commentary: We are a polyamorous Family and I encourage contact between my slave and Others. However, my slave's time is MY time and I must know how my slave is spending her time. By extension, I must know about these relationships both because any relationship consumes time and because any relationship involves emotions. In that light, I must be comfortable that my property is at no risk of psychological or physical damage and one way of monitoring the slave's well-being is to monitor both sides of all correspondence. When this has occurred in the past, my slave has made it clear to the other person that I must be copied on all e-mail. As a matter of practice, I release the other person from this requirement after I have a sense of the person's honor and integrity and only require my slave to keep me generally apprised of the relationship.

How to Ask a Question

When in protocol, the proper form for questions regarding any possible action by the slave is, "Sir, do you wish this slave to [description of action], Sir?"

It is immaterial if the word "wish" is replaced with "want," "desire," "intend", and so on. It is also immaterial if the action is simple (like going to the bathroom or answering the phone), or more complex (like getting ready to go out to theater), or a prelude to further conversation (asking if Master wishes the slave to tell Him something). What matters is that instead of the slave expressing his/her own desire and asking Master to approve or reject it (an accidental regression to an earlier time in the slave's life, to be sure), the slave presents a possibility *without becoming invested in it,* and awaits Master's decision.

> *Commentary: Living in obedience goes beyond doing only as you're told; it means that the slave also wants only what the slave's Master wants.*

How to Make a Response

As Master's response to the slave's question is effectively an order, the slave's response to any order, Instruction, acknowledgement, correction, explanation, or information conveyed by Master is, "Sir, yes, Sir, thank you, Sir!"

The same form is used whenever the slave answers a question in the affirmative. If the slave's answer is negative, then, "Sir, no, Sir, thank you, Sir!"

> **Commentary:** *There is a body of thought that proposes that the slave not be allowed to say "no," and instead, uses the construction: "Sir, only if it pleases you, Sir!" Here, the "only if" signals "no", but leaves the decision up to Master. Clearly, there are times when it would be nonsensical for the slave to use the "only if" construction. For example, if you asked your slave if there is a backup jar of applesauce in the pantry and the answer came back: "Sir, only if it pleases you, Sir," you might rightfully suspect that your rigid requirement for the use of structured language had gone too far.*

Occasionally, these forms may be varied by inserting, "Master" ("Sir, yes, Sir! Thank You, Master!"), but the basic form is invariant (life can be wonderfully simple when almost everything calls for the same response!)

> **Commentary:** *While the slave has no trouble replying to every sentence with: "Yes, Master" or "Yes, Sir," I have found it more difficult in everyday life to get my slave to use this more formal military structure with two "sirs" in the sentence. I have been lax in enforcing this, for I believe that in simplifying the response to "Yes, Sir", the slave fulfills the intent of the structure and that use of the more formal military wording is less important. Said differently, you have to pick your fights and this one strikes me as a trivial matter in the overall scheme of an M/s relationship.*
>
> *By the way, my slave is much better about using the two-Sir or two-Master sentence construction when we are in High Protocol.*

Extended Questions or Comments – High Protocol

Invoked only in High Protocol, if the slave feels the need to ask an involved question or one that will require more than a yes/no response from Master, the slave asks, "Sir, will you permit your slave to ask a question, Sir?"

Similarly, in High Protocol, if the slave feels the need to make a comment, the slave asks, "Sir, will you permit your slave to make a comment, Sir?" In both cases, the slave awaits Master's response, and says, "Sir, yes, Sir! Thank you, Sir!" whether the response is affirmative or negative, and, finally, if the response was affirmative, asks the question or makes the comment (beginning each sentence with "Sir" as usual and ending the last sentence with "Sir" as well).

Commentary: Each Master must decide how freely his/her slave is allowed to speak. The desire for the relationship to last is at the core of the M/s dynamic. If both Master and slave are introverts, this formality may be seen as a godsend (because it cuts down on the idle chatter that neither party would desire). On the other hand, if both Master and slave are extroverts, protocols that limit speech probably won't work. In my case, both my slave and I are "researchers" who would sometimes rather read than talk, so these restrictive protocols work well for us.

No Arguments

The slave is never wrong to ask for clarification of his/her orders, or to offer to inform Master of something that is troubling – or, for that matter, brings joy to the slave! Leading questions and argumentative expressions of opinion must be avoided. The slave is always to consider him or herself to be Master's property; a being wholly devoted to fulfilling Master's will.

At Master's discretion, Master and the slave may discuss any matter at all – but they do not argue!

Chapter 4

"How to Be" in Master's Presence

Protocols when in Master's Presence

The Master/slave Relationship is a special one. The number of successful BDSM M/s Households in the world is miniscule. The Protocols in this section celebrate the unusual nature of this dynamic; they call both for the Master and the slave to come present to their Relationship.

Note: Most of the material in this chapter – especially the two sections *Presenting/Continuing* and *Refinements in the Art of Service* – is based upon the protocols developed by Apex Academy/Butchmann's. As the original material has been so interlaced with my comments and our adapted versions of the original, it is not practical to supply quotation marks around each quoted line, but know that this material is mostly from that source. Again, I thank Master Steve Sampson for permitting their use in this book.

Coming Present before Beginning our Evening

The Master/slave relationship is extremely unusual in society. You may wish to recognize that difference with some form of daily ceremony, as I have done. *Coming together* after a day's absence (for example, when the slave has to work) or *coming together* on a weekend evening when we have been out of protocol all day, is marked by **ceremony**. The rest of this section presents the ceremony that we use. Obviously, you have to develop your own.

If returning from a day out of the house, the slave will enter the house, find Master, and assume the *full present* position. Master will welcome the slave, and – if something is planned for the evening that requires special dress – explain any special needs. This is NOT the time for our "recommitment ceremony," so, after this brief greeting the slave is released to attend to tidying the house, showering and dressing for dinner. [Note: Master will also dress and then retire to the living room to read while awaiting the slave's return. The slave will not interrupt before reappearing, fully dressed – discussed in Chapter 5.]

The slave's reappearance, Dressed, signals the start of our Evening; we are now in High Protocol, and we use all the formal speech and motion protocols.

The slave will seek out Master and assume the Full Present position and remain in this position until recognized. We now conduct our *Recommitment Ceremony*:

1. Master: "What have you brought me?"
2. slave: "Your slave, Master"
3. Master: "So it is. And what should I do with such a thing?"
4. slave: "Take me and keep me as yours, if it pleases you, Master."
5. Master: "And why should I do such a thing?"
6. slave: "Because you own me, Master, and because we love one another."
7. Master: "These are good reasons, and so I will accept you. You may rise."

Commentary: We go through this ritual every single day we are together, and have done so since my slave first accepted my collar. When I describe this in protocol presentations at conferences, I'm often asked why we do this, since we're clearly in a permanent relationship. We do this for a number of reasons. First, this is a time to talk out any upsets that have come to us this day. This is our "talk time" – a time when I probe my slave's mental and emotional state before we begin our Evening. If there are private things I wish to tell my slave, this is the time I do it. If my slave is upset about something, this is the time to discuss it. Said differently, this is a daily reality check into our relationship. (Timing note: if we have any "talking" to do, it is done before we start in on the recommitment ritual that appears in the box, above. I only begin our ritualized dialog after I'm assured that we don't have some emotional or fact-based issue hanging over us. That way, the balance of our evening can proceed without stress or drama.)

Coming Present after Being Together in Low Protocol All Day

Particularly on weekends, we will use "Dressing" as the point of demarcation between low protocol and the high protocol of our Evenings together. Master will inform the slave when to begin the bathing/changing process and how to dress for that evening. The "Recommitment Ceremony" follows once the slave has dressed.

Presenting/Continuing

In many M/s relationships, the ceremony of greeting and leaving is managed through Presenting. Here, the slave takes a specific position, pauses to feel his/her slavery, and awaits Master's acknowledgment. This act announces the slave's presence and readiness to obey. It is now that the slave awaits a specific order or an instruction to "continue." All these aspects of presenting are described in further detail, below. This section provides a glimpse of how "presenting" often works in a high protocol setting.

Entering and Leaving Master's Presence and Control

Because of the special kind of relationship shared between Master and slave, certain ritual reminders help the slave focus and reflect on the reality of the respective roles in your life together. For example, the slave will not say "Hello" to Master. As previously discussed, the slave is not a boyfriend or girlfriend. When the slave greets Master, the slave is surrendering to Master's control. Therefore, the greeting must be Special.

Similarly, when the slave takes leave of Master, the slave is requesting that Master's control be extended beyond his direct presence. Therefore, casual, familiar greetings and farewells are replaced by disciplined, thoughtful processes and rituals.

When to Present

The slave is expected to present:

- When the slave comes into or leaves Master's presence; thus, at any time when under social conditions a "Hello" or "Goodbye" would be appropriate.
- When the slave needs to ask a question of Master or receive additional instructions to complete an assigned task.
- When the slave has completed all currently assigned tasks and awaits Master's pleasure. The slave who has finished assigned tasks does not simply go off and do as the slave pleases, but instead, asks whether Master has other instructions. (If Master is not present, the slave should exert initiative in light of the slave's training and standing orders.)

When another slave presents in the same space, the slave never merely stands by and watches, but joins in the process by taking the Present position and holds it while awaiting Master's order to "continue." This rule underscores that all slaves are brothers/sisters and equals who support one another's slavery in any way possible.

The complete presenting ritual is not required when Master or slave comes and goes repeatedly in the course of normal household or other activities. However, if seated, the slave will ordinarily stand whenever Master enters the space the slave occupies and remains in the Standing Present position until told to "sit" or "continue."

When the slave who has recently presented to Master re-enters Master's space before completing those duties, he/she should simply complete these tasks as inconspicuously as possible and, once tasks are completed, assume a standing present position until given further instructions.

How to Present

By presenting, the slave brings him or herself within Master's awareness and waits for acknowledgement without disturbing whatever Master is doing. If it is Master who enters a space where the slave is engaged, the slave stops whatever he/she was doing and assumes a

Standing Present to indicate readiness to follow Master's direction.

Traditional Present Positions. The following formal positions commonly used in the Leather tradition express the strength of the slave and the power of the slave's obedience. With the exception of the Honor Present, all are held without moving until the slave is released by an order from the Master to whom the slave is presenting. The four positions may be modified in special circumstances (for instance, if the slave is on crutches or must use a wheelchair). When Master signals these positions the intent is to convey the message that we have moved into high protocol. This might occur in a public setting when we meet someone else from the Leather Tribe.

For graphic representations of the various *presentation* stances, see: http://ww.bearpair.com/Leather/Positions.htm

---

Full Present: The slave kneels upright (on both knees, not sitting on the heels). Knees are spread shoulder width apart, arms locked behind back, each hand clasping the opposite forearm (or wrist if the slave is incapable of grasping the forearm); chest is held forward, wide and strong; head bowed with eyes down. This is the default form and normally used whenever Master is sitting or lying down. [Note: I prefer eye contact from my slave, not a "head lowered" position.]

While you may want to use a different silent signal, I silently signal the slave to take this position by pointing my index finger towards the floor with two rapid downward motions.

Honor Present: The Honor Present is the same as the Full Present except only the right knee touches the ground and the left leg is bent. In either case, after the slave makes a greeting statement such as: "Sir, on behalf of my Master, I am honored to meet you." The slave stands again without waiting for a command. An Honor Present is used to greet a Leather Master or Guest – in public or in private – who might be embarrassed if the slave waits for an order to "continue."

Again, while you may wish to develop a different signal, I silently signal Honor Present by gesturing toward the floor with the flat of my hand, all fingers extended.

Standing Present calls for the slave to stand with legs shoulder-width apart, hands behind the back, each hand grasping the opposite forearm. This is used in private or in public Leather events as the default "attending" position.

I silently signal the "Standing Present" and "Public Present" positions by holding my arm slightly away from my body and pointing the index finger of my right hand forward and horizontal to the floor (not AT the floor) and then rotating my wrist 90-degrees, back and forth – pointing ahead, pointing to the right, pointing ahead, pointing to the right. The slave knows to perform the Standing Present when Master is standing and if we are in private or at a public Leather event. The slave knows I use the same hand signal to indicate *Public Present* when we are in public and we do not want to draw unwarranted attention to the kneeling position of a Full Present.

Public Present uses the same overall posture as "Standing Present," except that the hands are positioned in a manner that lets anyone behind the slave see the open palms held crossed behind the small of the slave's back, similar to a military "parade rest." As just mentioned, this is used in public when kneeling – or even the unusual arm positions of the Standing Present – might draw undesirable attention.

Commentary: While there may be other forms of Present and other hand signals used to invoke them, I have only listed those I use with my slave. You may have other positions and other signals that you wish to develop to meet your own particular situation.

Some Refinements in the Art of Service

Feeling the slave's Slavery

"After a slave is in a PRESENTING position, he or she pauses to feel the presence of their slavery. It is important for the slave to take the needed time for this – to feel the strength and dedication of their slavery, to let the rush and static of the outside world subside, and to find the peace of his slavery before addressing the Master." (Butchmann's: *Feeling your slavery*)

> *Commentary: I consider this point to be very important. I have observed instances where a slave has appeared almost insolent in the performance of service because the slave has made only perfunctory recognition of an action. That is, the slave will serve without focusing on the Honor of the service or without honoring the process of serving. For example, if I ask for a pen, I expect my slave to go and find a pen, bring it to me, move to Honor Present position, focus on the pen, place it in the palms of both hands, kiss the pen and offer it to me. I would be horrified if my slave were to say simply: "Oh, sure – here's a pen, Master," and pass the thing to me. In fact, that would be a serious show stopper. I would immediately put the slave in full present position and ask what is wrong, for in our world, something truly dreadful just happened.*

Waiting for Recognition

The slave must continue with the presenting ritual until Master recognizes the slave's presence by a word, look or gesture.

- If Master is busy and moving around the room when the slave enters and takes up a Standing Present position, then the slave's eyes move to follow Master's location in order to not miss a hand signal or gesture to approach.

- The slave may need to alter location in the room to ensure Master is always in eyesight. Typically, however, Master will quickly notice the slave and signal either to "sit," "stay," or "continue." If told to "stay," the slave remains in the Standing Present position until given another order.

Commentary: In our life together, one of the most annoying problems comes from hosting a party and not being able at all times to have use of my slave. Intellectually, I understand that my slave is working on something relevant to a guest or to the party as a whole. But, when the party is fairly small – say three other couples and there is no one to help my slave – I often find myself wishing for more backup. At any rate, this protocol describes the slave's behavior when checking in with me in that kind of setting.

Presenting in Special Situations

Presenting in a Restaurant. The slave stands at the end of the booth or at the side of the table in the Public Present position until Master signals the slave to sit by word or gesture. The slave discreetly says, "Sir, yes, Sir! Thank You, Sir!", and takes the indicated seat. If Master stands for any reason, the slave will again rise to the Public Present position – gracefully and naturally, not looking hurried, clumsy, or "put upon" – and remain in that position until Master gives a different direction.

Commentary: We live this lifestyle 24/7 and are seldom out of protocol.

Chapter 5

Rituals and Routines

Actions Preparatory to Master's Visit

State of the slave's Residence

The entire house will be tidy, with particular attention to the kitchen and bedroom. Nothing will be found on any surface other than what may be necessary for preparing the evening meal. The dining room table will be set and the book the slave is reading to me will be set out.

If seasonally appropriate, the slave will set the fireplace with adequate firewood and kindling, and ensure that the fireplace is ready to be lit.

Electric lighting will be subdued throughout the house, set to a pleasing orange glow (dimmer switches set at approximately half power). Glaring lights (kitchen or hallway) will be turned off. Candles and flowers will be placed on tables as appropriate.

Drinks and appetizers will have been prepared both for Master and the slave. These will be waiting (without ice) until Master arrives. Upon hearing Master's arrival, the slave will place ice in drinks.

Appetizers – such as smoked salmon, cheeses, fruits, crackers, etc. – will be prepared/arranged in an artistic manner.

> **Commentary:** *While you may use any etiquette guide that suits your levels of formality, I have relied heavily on* Service Etiquette*. 4th Ed. by Oretha D. Swartz. Annapolis, MD: Naval Institute Press, 1988, as the basis of our family Protocols.*
>
> *I am highly visual and sensitive to clutter; I notice the quality of objects. Taken together, I care a great deal about the look of my house and how it is maintained.*

Appropriate Dress

NOTE: I hesitate to include this section from my own *Manual of Protocol* because "appropriate dress" varies so between couples and depends upon the gender of the slave. When you write this section in your own manual, consider preparing protocols for different situations, such as...

- Dress for Informal Dinner
- Dress for Formal Dining-In

If you do not live in a 24/7 relationship, then...
- Dress if Master is Arriving for Dinner
- Dress if Master is Arriving after Dinner

Some hints: For male slaves, there are some times when you want the slave to be wearing chaps, other times that includes a chain harness, other times when it should be a leather harness, and so forth. For female slaves, there are some times when you want the slave dressed in lingerie or in a French maid's outfit, times when you want the slave nude, times you want the slave in harness, and so forth.

For my own (female) slave, we generally wear military mess dress for formal dinners, but my slave's standard dress around the house – day or night – calls for a black cincher with garters, black hose, heels and black bra.

At no time when the slave is Dressed may the slave wear underwear. [Note: It is my Instruction that if the slave wears underwear, it signals a desire to be scolded and spanked.]

State of the slave upon Master's Arrival

Physical Position: The slave will wait in Standing Present position far enough behind the front door to allow Master adequate entry without obstructing his ability to maneuver. Unless previously instructed otherwise, the slave will be dressed in black cincher, garters and black hose – as described above. The slave will drop down to Full Present as Master enters the door.

Mental State: The slave will be in a positive and up-beat mood, focused on being present. If there are special, *troubling issues,* the slave will have communicated these to Master **before** Master's arrival and they will be Attended To after this ceremony ends. If there is some serious issue (e.g.: death of a relative; serious personal illness) that will have a negative effect upon this *greeting ritual,* and if the slave has not been able to communicate this information to Master earlier in the day, the slave **must** tell Master immediately upon arrival.

Coming Present: At this point, we go through our *Recommitment Ceremony*, previously described.

> **Commentary:** *This section described the slave's prepara-tions for a visit FROM Master to the slave. The next section describes the slave's visit TO Master OR the slave's evening preparations when the slave lives with Master.*

Preparing Master's House for an "Evening"

Everything that applied to preparing the slave's house also applies when the slave has spent the day at Master's house. It is the slave's responsibility to carry out the final tidying and to personally prepare for the evening. In reality, I excuse the slave about 90 minutes before I wish to have cocktails, and the slave begins to prepare the evening meal, the drinks and appetizers, sets the house lighting levels (previously described as this related to the slave's house), lights the candles (after first trimming the wicks), turns on whatever music the slave has selected, and lights incense (if desired). The slave then showers and Dresses. Seasonally, I light the fireplace (that the slave previously prepared).

Coming Present: The slave next comes into my presence only when appropriately Dressed; we then go through our *Recommitment Ceremony*, previously described.

> **Commentary:** *This is another example of the sub-theme of this Manual/book: using the M/s dynamic as a vehicle to make every day special. We use Ceremony as the demarcation between the mundane part of life and the exceptionally special magic that we've built into our relationship.*

Dining

One way you can make the day *special* with your slave is to wrap the evening meal in protocol. I have endeavored to do that over the years and offer this chapter to you as a model for this form of scene. As I recognize that you may choose to alter portions of this and some of the following sections, I have written them in my own voice.

In our Family, most evening meals are semi-formal affairs. A series of customs and rituals have evolved that make these evenings special. This section covers Family decorum during these times. While most of the following comments relate to meals prepared and served at home, some references relate to behavior, actions or manners in public or at events given by others.

So, this part of the book details how to prepare the house and the meal in the style that I require. It explains how to set the table for the appropriate level of service and how to clear the table and clean the dishes. As there are myriad ways that readers may choose to structure their meal times to fit their preferred lifestyle, this section should be read only as a guide to the kinds of protocols you may wish to develop for your own situation.

Background
General Notes on Decorum: As a Family, it is our Policy to appear at home and away from home slightly *dressed up*. However, we do not seek to be conspicuous – just a little more dressed than is customary. This is also true about *behavior* and *speech*. For example, I support conventional behavior in public, better to blend with the surroundings. In terms of speech, I am sensitive to regional speech patterns my slave uses and have required that the slave eliminate them (In Texas: "I'd *like for* you to help me with this project", or "I'm *fixin' to* go to the store."). I also require my slave to correct regionally-induced grammatical errors ("There are three of them over there" is to be used, as opposed to, "There's three of them over there," that contains a subject-verb agreement problem).

Commentary: *One's dress, one's dialect/accent and one's articulation level telegraphs one's upbringing. If anyone wants an instant lesson in this, just watch women shopping at Sacs Fifth Avenue; listen to their speech. No, not everyone you see there will walk gracefully, nor speak fluidly with high-level language skills, but the sales clerks certainly notice the difference between those whose mannerisms are polished and refined, and those with less sophistication.*

Rationale – Why have "Dining Protocols"? Formal dining makes a ceremony out of the *eating experience.* My idea of an Exceptional Evening includes dressing up and having a gourmet meal before hours of play. As my slave's duty is to support my vision, this section describes that vision in detail.

Dining in; Dining out
I have adapted terms used to describe formal military meal service.

> **Dining In** is the term I use to refer to *formal or semi-formal* evening meals served to Family only.

> **Dining Out** is the term I use to refer to *formal or semi-formal* evening meals that also include non-Family members.

The slave will keep a notebook of meals served for all Guests at Dining Out events. Notes will include wines served, as well as the foods for each course. The slave will record all gifts brought by Guests and is responsible for preparing written thank-you notes for Master to send.

How "Formal" is this? If you read books on formal service, you will immediately realize that a true formal dinner requires a serving staff. The serving staff does *not* eat with the Host and Guests. Because I wish to eat my meals *with* my slave(s), I have modified certain aspects of the *formal dining* service to account for periods when slaves are seated at Table.

In traditional formal service, no serving platters or bowls are passed between seated guests, as they would be at a "family style" meal. While my slave or others in service to me through my slave will take the serving dishes to each guest at the beginning of each course, occasions *do* arise when a condiment (such as gravy or cranberry sauce) will be needed again. Passing these from one person to another avoids any significant interruption in the flow of the dinner conversation. Once my slave has served the course to Master and each guest, and is then seated at the table, the slave's remaining duty is closely to monitor water glass and wine glass levels and to take the initiative to keep them refilled.

Personal Table and Dinner Party Decorum and Manners

Note: You can read this section in two ways. First, these two pages can serve as an *orientation memo* that you include in dinner invitations to guests; second, it serves as your House Guide to personal manners for your Family members when you and they are dining at the home of another person.

Dining Tips for High Protocol Dinners

Please turn off your cell phone before entering the house. Our evening will start with appetizers and drinks, and we will then move to the dining room for dinner. You will approach your chair from the left side (and when you get up at the end of the dinner, you will leave your chair from the right side).

Once at Table, please remain silent and respectful throughout the "Coming Present" ceremony my slave and I will share before we eat. At a formal dinner, slaves and submissives will rise as they see their Masters (or Doms) rise.

These are tips for the period before dinner is served:

- Drinks, including hard liquor beverages, may be served before dinner. Hard liquor is never consumed during the meal, and any remaining beverage left in your glass when dinner is served should not be brought to Table.

- Do not attempt to converse with the service slaves while they are actively in service at the beginning of each course. This is likely to distract them from their duties.

These are tips for properly handling wine and the offering of Toasts:

- Don't touch your wine glass until Master offers the opening Toast.

- Hold your red wine glass by the bowl, not by the stem; white wine, hold the stem, not the bowl (you don't want to warm the chilled white wine).

- When the Master rises to give the toast, guests are also expected to rise.

- The exception is, when you are being toasted individually, you remain seated.

- Don't offer a toast while someone else is toasting until after everyone drinks to that toast.

- It's considered good manners to ask the host for permission before proposing a toast of your own.

- Recognize your rank and be sure that when you raise your glass in toast, the edge of your glass remains lower than those of higher rank to you.

- Do not clink wine glasses, as you could inadvertently shatter a crystal goblet.

- Cut only one piece of food before eating it.

- When you are not using your utensils, place them diagonally across the dinner plate's upper right edge.

- The knife blade is turned to face the center of the plate.

- When you have finished eating, place your utensils flat, diagonally across the upper 1/3 of the plate, food end pointing towards 11 and hand end pointing at 3.

Managing your napkin.

- Do not touch your napkin until Master places her/his napkin in her/his lap.

- Do not fully unfold the napkin – open it to the point where it's folded in half, the folded side towards your body.

- If you have to leave Table before the meal has ended, place your napkin on your chair.

- Master will signal the end of the meal by placing his napkin on the table and indicating that it is time to clear off the table.
- At the end of the meal, place the folded napkin to the right of the dinner plate.
- Under no circumstances do you place the linen napkin on the dirty plate.

Terms and Serving Protocols within This Family
Master is served first. The slave will act as Alpha slave and supervise any submissive in his/her charge. Such submissives will serve Master at his slave's direction. Whomever is serving will, upon completing that service, serve him/herself. (Note: Serving protocols when non-family members are present are covered in a later discussion of the "Order of Precedence.")

Timeliness when Invited to a Party
One of the most valuable habits that anyone can acquire is that of being on time. In our Family, we will arrive within 15 minutes of the specified starting time, particularly for a dinner party. We will not arrive before the stated start time.

Leaving a Party
Formal dinner parties often have a *guest of honor,* who will be announced when other guests are invited. In these situations, we will never leave the party before this Guest. Similarly, we will avoid staying longer than 15 minutes after the guest of honor has left.

If a member of our Family is the guest of honor, we will remain no more than 30-45 minutes after dinner is concluded. If there is no guest of honor, we will not remain longer than an hour after dinner is concluded.

Expressing your Thanks
Any Family member who has been a guest at a party or a dinner is expected to write or telephone the host or hostess. That is, while a sincere expression of thanks when leaving the party is generally suf-

ficient, when participating in a High Leather Protocol dinner party, something more formal than a casual "thanks" is called for. After a special affair, the Host would be pleased to hear that you enjoyed the hospitality, and a note or phone call is in order.

Breakfasts and Luncheons

Breakfast – Routine
The slave will ask Master what he would like prepared for breakfast. With rare exceptions, the meal will be bacon and eggs that the slave will prepare and serve on the informal breakfast table. This meal is prepared as follows:

Freshly brewed coffee: Start brewing the coffee before anything else. Preparation: nine heaping tablespoons of ground coffee per 12-cup coffee maker. When brewing is complete, pour into a cup, ¾ full and add powdered creamer to obtain a beige color. The coffee is poured into the cup after the bacon and eggs are served.

Two strips of bacon done medium well: Place bacon on three folded sheets of paper towel, cover with one folded sheet of paper towel and microwave for three minutes, or until crisp and greaseless. Place the bacon neatly (in relation to the scrambled eggs) on breakfast plate.

Two scrambled eggs, seasoned as follows: four squirts of "Liquid Smoke;" a few squirts of hot sauce of choice (I tend to prefer Louisiana Hot Sauce™); a little Lowery's™ seasoned pepper. Cook eggs medium dry and place them attractively on the breakfast plate with garnish (parsley and/or tomato) as decoration.

Breakfast – Holiday
Holiday breakfasts, prepared by slave(s), are served on the formal dining room table, rather than on the informal kitchen table. Special Holiday table decorations will be in order: consult Master.

Flatware usually includes only knife, fork and teaspoon. If coffee is served in a mug, the teaspoon is placed to the right of the knife. If coffee is served in a coffee cup that rests in a saucer, the teaspoon is placed on the saucer.

Dishes are pre-warmed on a plate warmer. Unlike formal dinners, foods are placed on the table and passed among the diners.

Holiday Breakfast Menu 1:

- **French toast:** One egg per two pieces of bread. Blend the eggs, sugar, maple extract, cinnamon and milk into a square glass cooking vessel and use a fork to blend it into a dipping batter for the bread.

- **Condiments:** chopped pecans; powdered sugar; real maple syrup that has been warmed in the microwave oven. [Note: Be careful when heating syrup, it will easily overheat and overflow the bottle. Remove cap from syrup container and microwave in 45-second bursts, closely monitoring syrup temperature.]

- **Two strips of bacon**, medium well done (if Others are dining with us, prepare their bacon in the manner each prefers.)

- **Whipped cream:** Place mixing bowl and blender blades AND the whipped cream in the freezer 20 minutes before preparing. To stabilize whipped cream, add 2 tablespoons of nonfat dry milk to every cup of whipping cream before you whip it. Add 2 Tbls powdered sugar and 2 tsp MAPLE extract once the cream starts to set up. Whip until mixture will hold a hard peak. Place in a serving bowl with a serving spoon.

  [*A few additional whipped cream notes*: Soupy whipped cream can be saved by adding an egg white, then chilling thoroughly and re-beating it. Adding a few drops of lemon juice to whipping cream reduces the whipping time. Whipping cream will not separate if you add ¼ tsp. unflavored gelatin per cup of whipped cream.]

- **Fresh coffee**

- **Orange juice;** Master requires ¼ tsp Sweet-N-Low™ added to his orange juice: stir.

Holiday Breakfast Menu 2:

- **Eggs,** prepared in various ways – Benedict, scrambled; fried; poached
- **Condiments** and accessories
- **Two strips of bacon**, done medium well
- **Freshly brewed Coffee**
- **Orange juice**

Lunch vs. Luncheon

There are actually arcane rules that govern the use of the terms "lunch" "lunched" and "luncheon." Correct usage is: "Yesterday I lunched with Master Andrew;" "We should prepare lunch;" "We are having a summer luncheon."

While you can say: "Lunch is served," it is somewhat *more correct* to use "luncheon." However, to avoid sounding stiff and pretentious, "luncheon" may be reserved for special events, thus: "The holiday luncheon is served." At any rate, it's hard to think of a "luncheon" comprised of a peanut butter and jelly sandwich, thus:

> *A two-course summer luncheon* is comprised of fruit or seafood served with salad, followed by dessert.

> *A three-course luncheon* can include soup, main course and dessert **or** main course, salad and dessert, **or** fruit (melon or grapefruit), main course and dessert, **or** casserole, salad and dessert, **or** soufflé, salad and dessert.

A few words about soup. First, there are three general types of soups and they are served differently:

- Clear soups (or broths such as bouillon), are served in a two-handled cup, with matching plate. Clear soups are eaten with a spoon that is round with a short handle. After the bouillon or clear soup has cooled, it is appropriate to lift the cup with both hands and drink from it.

- Thicker forms of soup are placed in a shallow wide-rimmed soup bowl and eaten with a spoon that is oval.

- Gumbo is eaten with a spoon that is round with a longer handle than the spoon used for a clear soup.

Second, when soup is served at a *formal* table, it is usually placed on the table after the guests are seated. When soup is served at an *informal* table, it is placed in front of the slave – who is responsible for serving it.

Sherry often accompanies the soup course and may be the only wine served at that time. A white or red wine, or both, may be offered at formal luncheons. Iced tea is placed on a coaster on the summer table after guests are seated. The iced-tea spoon is placed to the right of the knives or above the plate at an informal meal. After the spoon is used, the bowl of the spoon is placed on the coaster. When hot tea is served, the service is the same as for coffee.

Second portions are NOT offered at a formal luncheon.

Preparations for Dining In or Dining Out

Special Preparations for Guests

Before planning the menu, the slave will contact the submissives/ slaves of each guest invited to a Dining Out to ascertain any drink or dietary preferences, including food allergies. The slave will also verify the name preferences and name spelling for guests in order to correctly prepare name place cards.

Although the order of service has been discussed in detail for "Dining In" conditions, the service order changes once guests have been invited. This is because a senior Leatherman would outrank Master as Head of Family, so far as the order of serving is concerned. Thus, Master will prepare an **Order of Precedence** chart (described later), so the slave knows how to set out the name place cards and also the order in which each person at Table is to be served.

Preparing the House
Living Room: Furniture is not out-of-place; those items that normally belong on a table or shelf are in their proper place, fireplace is set; every table lamp or oil lamp is either turned on or lit; additional candles are lit; all light-levels adjusted to an orange color cast; all flower arrangements are correct and vases are cleaned and filled with fresh water.

Kitchen: all dishes are clean and put away; counters are spotless and sanitized; floors have been swept and washed; sink is scoured; everything stored in its proper place.

Dining Room: centerpiece is in place, place cards are in place (name spellings have been checked previously with any Guests); condiments have been placed on the table.

Throughout the house, be sure all waste paper baskets have been emptied, that there is adequate toilet paper in all bathrooms, that there is adequate facial tissue throughout the house and that all appears orderly and tidy.

Setting the Table
General Rules
- Verify that all silver is polished.

- The tablecloth and napkins should be snow white or perhaps pastel colored to provide a simple background on which to present the food. (Personal note: we often use a black table cloth on top of a larger white lace tablecloth. I find the layering effect to be elegant and I prefer using a black table cloth in all but the most formal of meals.)

- Wine glasses should be clear and uncolored in order to best appreciate the subtle color of the wine.

- Dinner plates, whether formal or everyday, white or colored, should not be highly decorated. One cannot appreciate the appearance of the food if one is distracted by complicated patterns.

- Table Decorations: According to most etiquette books, the basic formal table centerpiece is a china, silver, or porcelain bowl or tureen filled with flowers and flanked by silver candelabra or four candlesticks. For small tables, consider a single flower placed by each plate.

  In our Family, we sometimes lay a single red carnation directly on the tablecloth, parallel with the edge of the table, centered above each dinner plate. For Special Dinners, we use red roses as opposed to carnations.

- Place cards are another hallmark of the formal dinner. As previously discussed, the slave is responsible for verifying that all guest name spellings have been verified and that these cards are correctly placed in relation to the rank of each Guest – as listed on the Order of Precedence sheet (described later).

The Place Setting
You can easily find diagrams of formal place settings on the Internet. While your slave may not be called upon to prepare such an event, such diagrams serve as a reference resource in order to correctly select and place flatware and stemware even on a less formal table.

Ambiance
In general, flowers improve the look of the table. Elaborate floral arrangements are THE hallmark of a formal dinner. However, take care not to block one guest's view of another guest with the flower arrangement. If dining at a small table, a small floral arrangement or a bowl of mixed fruit may serve as the centerpiece – or place single flowers in individual vases at each place.

Candlelight adds intimacy to a dinner. The size and style of the candlesticks depend on the occasion itself, but they should never be too grandiose.

Cutlery 201
Precise rules govern the positions of cutlery placement, whether you are serving with stainless steel or with silver. First, for knives and forks, there is a distinction between luncheon and dinner flatware. Dinner knives and forks are slightly larger and heavier than their luncheon

counterparts. In a general way, flatware is laid on the table according to use, starting on the outside of the place setting and working toward the plate. Forks are placed to the left of the plate, except that seafood forks are placed to the *right of the spoon, tines up.*

A fork is provided for each course unless one is expected to eat the course with a spoon. (Any time you're uncertain, copy the host or hostess.) The usual flatware placement presumes that the salad is a first course (informal dinner). So, if the meal includes salad, main, and dessert courses served in this order, the salad fork, dinner fork, and dessert fork will be placed in the same order to the left side of the dinner plate. When salad is served following the main course (formal dinner), the salad fork is placed next to the plate.

The various knives are placed immediately to the right of the plate, also in the order of the dish being served, from the outside toward the inside. Salad and dessert knives are provided if they're likely to be needed for cutting tomatoes or wedges of lettuce in the salad course or fruit in the dessert course. The spoons are placed to the right of all the knives, again in the order of the courses for which they're needed, again from the outside toward the inside.

Teaspoons or place spoons (larger) on the informal luncheon or dinner table are used for soup served in cups or for fruit. Teaspoons on the breakfast table are for grapefruit, cereals, and the like. Before serving tea or coffee, teaspoons are placed on the saucers at the right of the handles. At **formal dinners**, dessert spoons and/or forks are brought in on the dessert plate. Fork on the left, spoon on the right. At **informal meals,** the dessert spoon and/or fork may be placed on the table, centered above the dinner plate.

An exception is made for utensils, such as the iced tea spoon, because it might be needed throughout the meal, and thus, remains to the left of all other spoons. Utensils specific to each course are removed at the end of the course.

Tableware 201
If you like to provide a bread plate (required at a formal dinner), this should be placed to the left of the fork with the individual butter

spreader placed across the top edge of the bread plate. If you are serving antipasto (an appetizer usually consisting of an assortment of foods such as smoked meats, cheese, fish, and vegetables), provide a side plate on top of the dinner plate. If beginning with pasta, place a smaller dish on top of the dinner plate; this will serve as the pasta plate.

At the end of a course, plates are removed from the left and clean plates are placed from the right.

Stemware 201

More good wine has been ruined by a malodorous glass than anything else. The slave will always **smell** a glass before placing it on the dining room table. Wine glasses have two common causes of bad smells: insufficient rinsing that leaves a detergent or chlorine smell, or absorption of environmental odors such as the scent of wood from the cupboard, cardboard from a storage box, or cooking odors. The slave will re-wash, or at least rinse out any glass if a bad odor is detected.

Stemware is placed above and to the right side of the plate. If more than one drink is served to each person, position each piece of glassware along a line slanting slightly towards the dinner knife. The dessert and the glass for the wine accompanying the dessert may also be brought to the table together. Stemware is arranged in order of use, starting from the right. Thus, the first glass is always the water glass, then the various wine glasses arranged according to the order that they will be used with the various courses.

Please see Appendix C for a resource concerning wine selection as a function of the food being served. From there, you can derive the type of wine glasses that will be set out.

For example, the order that follows presumes that a fruit or fish dish will be followed by a meat dish and that a dessert will be served.

- Water
- White wine.
- Red wine
- Dessert wine

Table Service – Details

Table Linen: The traditional formal dinner table is covered with a white or ivory-colored damask tablecloth. A silence pad should be placed over the table and under the tablecloth. A lace or linen table-cloth for formal dining affairs must not overhang the edge of the table. Linen placemats may be used on top of the tablecloth.

Napkins: Napkins should match the table linen service. In formal dining, white and off-white napkins are used; one doesn't wish to detract from the place settings. If the china is solid white, take care that the napkin color is complimentary. Napkin size varies with the function:

- 24" square — very formal dinner
- 18-22" square — less formal multi-course meal
- 12" x 20" (called "lapkins") are for a buffet service where a one-dish menu is eaten from the lap
- 14-16" square — luncheon service
- 12" square (held under a tea plate) — used for afternoon tea
- cocktail napkins — when folded properly in quarters, are about 1/3rd the size of the luncheon napkin

Table China: It is customary for all plates used at one time to match. That is, one may change out the pattern of plates between the main course and the dessert course if the plates don't come from the same pattern.

Chargers: Chargers are decorative elements that are placed underneath plates to add color or texture to the table. Each plate should be set in the center of the place setting and place settings should be set equidistant from each other. The rest of the components used to set a formal table will be set with the dinner plate in mind. The charger will generally be removed just before the main course. Note: If a charger is used, soup and melon bowls will be placed on top of it. Then the entire setting (charger and soup or melon bowls) will be removed before the next course is presented.

Water Pitcher: Water is frequently overlooked by those unused to providing more formal dinners. The water pitcher – made of cut glass – is an item for the table that contributes to the air of formality. Be sure that all water glasses – and the water pitcher – are filled just before everyone is seated. The pitcher of water should remain on the table throughout the meal.

Serving Dishes: The sizes of serving dishes and platters vary as a function of the number of guests you intend to serve routinely. You will generally need serving dishes appropriate to serve the following.

- Vegetable dishes
- Soft dishes such as fruit compote (bowl required)
- Fruits and desserts (shallow bowl required)
- Bread tray or basket
- Sauceboat or gravy boat
- Small oval platter for meats or fish
- Large oval platter for large roasts (or cold meats at a buffet)
- Round platter or cake-stand (a cake plate on a pedestal) for serving pies, cakes, cookies etc.

Salt and Pepper: It is a hallmark of a formal dinner that each guest have individual saltcellars at their place setting. (Note to readers: check out eBay for saltcellars – also: salt cellars.)

Wine caddy: Wine bottles are placed in a wine caddy, not directly on the tablecloth. This is done to avoid an errant drip of wine falling onto the fine table linen. If serving chilled wines, a wine bucket is set on the sideboard table. The wine bucket must be placed on a plate in order to protect the wooden sideboard from getting wet from the condensate that will drip from the sides of the iced bucket.

Pre-seating Preparation:
Our pre-seating checklist follows:

Table-Check Checklist	Yes?
Candles are of sufficient length to last throughout the dinner – change if necessary.	
Everything *silver* upon the table is adequately polished – polish if necessary.	
Silver wine caddy is on the table and that the evening's bottle of dinner wine is placed upon it.	
Verify that the dinner setting (both the plate and silverware) are ONE INCH from table's edge.	
If the forks are placed on a napkin, that napkin must be one inch from table's edge	
Verify that place cards have been correctly placed in relation to the rank of each Guest and that all guest name spellings have been checked.	
Verify that there is no errant candle wax that has dripped onto the candle holder	

Checklist of Items Placed on or Near the table	Yes?
Apple sauce or mint jelly or cranberry sauce	
Salt/pepper	
Filled water glasses	
Open bottle of wine	
Place a full water pitcher on the sideboard	
If salad dressing is to be applied by diners AT the table, then this dressing must be placed on the table before diners are seated	

Special Conditions	
Be sure to open all red dinner wines at least 30 minutes before dinner is to be served	
If any diners prefer grape juice to wine, their glasses must be filled before the Call to Dinner.	
If salad is to be served, salad plates will be placed in the freezer when dinner preparation begins.	

Menus
(As a footnote to history, in the Military Services, the traditional *formal meal* includes standing prime rib roast and Yorkshire pudding.)

Four courses:
- Seafood cocktail (white wine)
- Soup
- Entrée (red wine)
- Cheese and fruit (dessert wine)

Five courses:
- Seafood cocktail (white wine)
- Soup
- Entrée (red wine for meat, white wine for fish)
- Salad
- Cheese and fruit (dessert wine)

Matching wine to the food course (see also Appendix C)

Sequence of Courses	Wine
Shrimp cocktail	White Burgundy*
Soup – usually clear	Sherry
Fish, hot or cold	White Rhine*
Main course of meat and vegetables	Merlot or claret
Main course of game and vegetables	Burgundy
Salad	No new wine
Dessert (ice cream, sherbet, etc)	champagne*
Fresh fruit (pears, grapes, etc)	champagne*
* serve chilled	

Wine Serving Temperatures
Wine service is as much art as science. Professional advice instructs that wines should be offered at the following temperatures, depending upon the kind of wine:

Type of Wine	Temperature in Degrees-Fahrenheit
"Young" whites	50-53
"Mature" whites	53-57
Rosé	50-57
Most reds	61-65
Sparkling wines	50-53
Sweet wines	50-65

Rolls, Coffee, Mints
- While bread is optional, rolls are always served at formal dinners. However, using bread plates for rolls is optional and depends upon space at Table.
- Coffee is always served at formal dinners.
- Mints are frequently served after the final course.

Cocktail and Appetizer Service Protocols

Serving Cocktails
The slave will be gloved when serving drinks. Drinks will be placed on a serving tray when brought into a room. Drinks will be arranged on the tray such that Master's drink is placed forward of all other drinks. Before drinks are offered to any Guest, the slave will offer a drink to Master from a *Full Present* position. Drinks are then offered to Guests from the tray according to the Order of Precedence previously prepared for the slave's use (and described later in this book).

Serving Wine
Mentioned previously, it is important to give the wine bottle a rotating twist at the very end of the pouring cycle to ensure a dripless result.

The slave will pour a small amount of wine into Master's glass. Master will sample the wine and signal whether to continue filling his glass or reject the bottle and open another. Once Master's glass has been filled, the slave will continue filling glasses according to the Order of Precedence.

Serving Appetizers

Servers will be gloved when serving appetizers. The slave will serve Master first from a Full Present position, then serve Guests. If the slave has another submissive present, the slave will only serve Master, then signal the additional helper to serve Guests.

Dressing for the Evening

Levels of Dress

Family events call for one of six levels of dress.

1) Family dress: Casual: think "shopping at the mall." Blue jeans are acceptable. Khakis (for men) are preferred. Clothing should be starched and pressed.

2) Silks: May be worn before 6 PM. For men: black dress slacks (wool preferred) and long-sleeved silk shirt or dress shirt with open neck. An ascot would be appropriate; jacket is optional. For women: anything classy that would be appropriate in public.

3) Fetish dress: Any fetish clothing that is less formal than military Mess Dress. For example, women could wear dressy lingerie: bra, garter belt, hose and heels.

4) Mess Dress: May not be worn before 6 PM; men will wear a short-wasted mess dress service jacket: Mess Dress, when worn with a standard pleated semi-formal shirt with collar, gold links, studs and black bow tie is called Mess Dress Blue by the military. As this applies to the Family, Master wears the Mess Dress tunic, but is generally shirtless. My slave wears a black Mess Dress uniform with black garter belt and hose with black stiletto heels.

5) Evening dress – Black tie – or Evening Mess Dress (worn with a stiff bodice, wing collar formal shirt, white bow tie, white vest, and pearl links and studs) may not be worn before 6 PM. Black tuxedo jacket or white tuxedo jacket are appropriate. For women, black suit jacket, black garter belt, black hose, black stiletto heels. Long black skirt is optional.

6) Full formal – White tie and tails. Boutonnieres other than white or red carnations may be worn in the left buttonhole. After 6 PM, except during the summer: Tails for men and floor-length black gown for women.

7) Family Ceremony – Cutaway jackets (gray) are mainly worn by the Family at special Family ceremonies.

Boutonnieres
Boutonnieres are NOT routinely used within our Family. (As an aside, do NOT wear a boutonniere when wearing military decorations.)

Dress Handkerchief
Family Protocols call for a red or black silk handkerchief used with tuxedo and tails – this is an optional item. However, our formal dress protocols in a vanilla setting call for a dress handkerchief that is white (this handkerchief may be initialed with a single letter or with all of one's initials. For evening use, the initials are white, gray or black.) Other handkerchief colors may be worn during the day and, if chosen, should blend with one's tie.

Gloves
During serving rituals: the slave(s) will wear white cotton service gloves during all serving rituals – drinks or food. In order to begin serving, the slave will wear white gloves immediately after our *Coming Present* ceremony when Mess Dress, Evening Dress or Full Formal Dress is worn.

Medals and Awards
Our Family may, from time to time, provide a medal as an Award for Service or Accomplishment. Regular size medals are worn with semi-

formal dress. Miniature medals are worn with mess dress, semiformal dress and dress whites. Ribbons are worn with Mess Dress, Evening Dress and Full Formal.

Dining Protocols

Rules Governed by the Level of Service

Formal Plated Service means that the slave will serve from left and remove from left. The slave will serve one plate at a time using the left hand. If the slave must serve a condiment, it is important to carry only one condiment at a time. This is gloved service.

Informal Plated Service means that the slave will serve from left, remove from right. In this case, the slave will approach the table carrying two full dinner plates, walk between two seated guests and first serve the guest to the right with the plate held in the right hand, then serve the guest on the left with the plate held in the left hand. Once everyone has been served their main course, the slave will return to the table bearing trays of condiments, one in each hand. In this case, the slave will offer these condiments to guests one at a time, offering first the bowl in the slave's right hand, then the bowl in the slave's left hand. This is ungloved service.

Rules Governing Table Service

Essentials of Service: Service at Formal Table must be efficient, quiet and unobtrusive. Nothing is ever taken directly from a slave's hands.

- If a guest is being brought something that the guest will take from the slave and place on the table, then the slave will bring that item to table on a serving tray. That tray is held with the right hand centered underneath the tray (right = submissive side) with the slave's left hand at the side [Note: This is the opposite of traditional formal service, where the tray is carried in the *left* hand. Never one to be troubled by inconsistency, we'll switch back to the traditional service mode in a few paragraphs.]

- If a guest is being brought something that will be transferred from a bowl onto the guest's plate, the slave may hold that bowl in gloved hands while the guest serves him or herself.

Rules of Service – initial course, plated service – formal meal. When the slave places the initial plate in front of the Guest, it is presented from the guest's left side using the slave's *left* hand (because of the angle of service). The plate rests in the palm of the slave's gloved hand and while using the right hand to effect the plate's transfer from the left palm to the place setting. [Note: in traditional formal service, the dish or platter rests on a folded napkin placed on the flat of the servant's ungloved hand. We do NOT follow that protocol because the slave is wearing gloves.]

Changing courses – plated service, formal meal. To ensure gracefulness, our protocol for changing plates during a course change involves two steps rather than the traditional one step. First, the slave removes the used plate from the table, placing it on the empty portion of the tray held by an assistant. Next, the slave removes a fresh plate from the same tray and, placing it in the palm of the left hand, now places it before the guest.

Note #1: If the slave is serving alone, then we're back to the traditional single one-step process: the slave carries the fresh dish in the *right* hand and after using the *left* hand to remove the used dish, places the fresh dish before the guest.

Note #2: We've had to revert to the traditional use of the right hand to carry the new dish because right-handed people would find it easier to stabilize a full plate using their strongest hand.

Changing Courses – plated service, informal meal. Two dishes are removed at one time and two fresh dishes are brought to Table at one time.

Changing Courses – two servers. My slave's assistant will stand with a large tray containing the plated next course and sufficient room to place a used dish; my slave (formally called *the table server*) will place a used dish on tray and then remove a fresh dish from the tray and place it in front of Guest.

The table linen is cleared of crumbs before dessert. A "crumber" will be used for this task (again, eBay is the source for table crumbers). The slave will hold the crumb tray below the table level to the left of the Guest and use the crumber brush to sweep the table surface to remove the offending object(s). Place cards are also removed at this time.

Dinner Seating Protocols

Starting Time. The starting time for dinners will usually be 8 PM, but this is at Master's sole discretion. Master will signal the time to begin moving to the dining room and then escort the appropriate person to the dining room. If this is a *Dining Out*, then the most senior guest will be the *appropriate person* to be escorted to Table.

How to Take your Chair Once it's your Turn to Do So. All dinner guests will be seated from the left side of the chair and will rise from their seats from the right side of the chair.

Who Sits First? Female Masters will be treated as male Masters, however Master will seat any Guest Femme Domme. Master will then signal other Doms/Masters to be seated, but Master will remain standing. When it comes to submissives, guest submissives will be seated after all their Doms/Masters have been seated. Master will specifically seat his slave, after which Family submissives will be seated in order of their rank/seniority, the most junior being the last to sit.

What Happens Next? Once everyone has been seated, Master will conduct his *"Centering Ritual."* This takes place before napkins are placed in the lap.

Centering **Ritual**: This ritual occurs before Master takes his seat. It is conducted so that the recipient can feel the special moment of this repast. It is a time of special bonding between Master and his submissives. It is important that all Family and Guests are utterly silent during this phase of the dinner rituals. Master will engage in his "Centering Ritual" with all Family submissives who are *at table* in order of their seniority.

[Note: I'm not going to describe this ritual. You are invited to make up your own or ask me via e-mail.]

When the ritual is over, Master will then take his seat and place his napkin in his own lap as a signal that everyone else may then remove their own napkins from table and place them in their laps. **This is also the signal for the slaves who are serving to rise and begin that process.**

Dinner Napkin Protocols
Napkin Handling: At the beginning of a meal, everyone puts their napkin in their laps, folded in half – not fully opened. The fold of the napkin is closest to your body, not your knees. During the meal, if you have to leave the table, place your napkin in your chair. At the end of a meal, place your napkin to the right of your dinner plate. *Be careful not to place your napkin ON your used dinner plate.*

How to Know the Meal has Ended: When Master has placed his napkin on the table the meal has ended.

Dinner Service Protocols
Order of Precedence: In designing the Order of Precedence chart, there are at least two possibilities:

1) To seat the next highest ranking person to the right of the highest ranking person, and the third highest ranking person right of the second highest, etc., and continue until the person of lowest rank sits left of the highest ranking person, or

2) To begin by placing the second highest ranking person to the right of the highest ranking person, then put the third highest ranking person to the left of the highest ranking person, and continue alternating to the left and right until the lowest ranking person is positioned furthest from the highest ranking.

Master will determine the seating pattern and provide the slave with the typed list.

Commentary: In my Household, we prefer the first table seating method, because it's much easier for the slave to pour wine into glasses when he or she can move smoothly around the table in a counter-clockwise fashion. If you seat according to the second method, the slave will have to cross back and forth around the table in order to serve in order of seniority (see the next section that addresses this issue).

Serving and Removing Plates: As previously noted, if this is an *informal* diner, the slave will serve from left, remove from right. If this is a **formal** dinner, then the slave will serve from left and remove from left. In either case, drinks – water and wine – are served and refilled from the RIGHT.

When a plated dish is placed before a diner, the slave will rotate the plate in such a way to ensure that the meat course is at 6 o'clock (closest to the seated diner).

Refilling a Glass with Water or Wine: Refill a **water glass** by picking up the glass and adding the water/ice while the glass is positioned over the carpet to the right and slightly behind the guest. Refill a **wine glass** by pouring the wine into the glass where it sits on the table – do **NOT** pick up the wine glass. If a left-handed person moves their glass (or glasses) to the left side of the table setting, the slave may pour from their left side to avoid reaching across them. Some people may hold the glass up to pour: watch out for this because an accident may occur.

Serving Protocols:

Pouring Wine: The slave always pours the wine, whether or not an assisting slave is present. This is solely my slave's honor. My slave will wear gloves and have a white linen kitchen cloth over the left forearm with which to address any accidental spills. As previously mentioned, when wine is poured, it is important to give the bottle a rotating twist at the very end of the pouring cycle to ensure that no dripping occurs. The slave will pour a small amount of wine into Master's glass. As previously mentioned, Master will sample the wine and signal whether to continue filling his glass or reject the bottle and open another. Once Master's glass has been filled, the slave will continue filling glasses according to the Order of Precedence, filling his/her own glass last. The slave will then be seated while the slave's own submissive begins the food service. If sherry glasses are used during the first course, they are removed after the salad course by the slave or (if available) by the slave's submissive. Other wine glasses remain on the table throughout the meal.

Serving Food – Non-Plated Meal: The slave will be gloved and will first serve Master from a kneeling position, then serve Guests by remaining standing and by lowering the served item within range of the guest's plate. The slave will position serving utensils within easy reach of the person being served. If the slave has a submissive present, the slave will serve only Master, then be seated and signal his/her submissive to serve the remaining Family members and/or Guests in order of precedence.

Beginning the Dinner

Summary of the Process of Starting Dinner:

- Everyone moves from the living room to the dining room upon the signal from Master.

- Master first seats the most senior Femme Domme present (Not-Leather) and then seats his slave. Other Masters and Doms take their seats. Remaining submissives take their seats.

- Everyone remains silent as Master performs the *Centering Ritual* with his slave and with any other Family submissives present.

- The slave rises and begins to serve food. At a formal meal, the slave's submissive will now be given the signal from my slave to rise from his/her seat and begin food service.

- After the food is served, Master first offers an appropriate Toast. Once these Toasts are completed, Master may offer another toast or ask an Honored Guest to offer a toast. Note: the toast may be a seated or standing toast depending upon the formality of the event.

- Master removes the napkin from its place on the table and puts it in his/her lap; everyone else takes this as their signal to remove their napkins from the table and put it in their laps.

How to Hold Wine and Liquor Glasses: The thumb and first two fingers at the base of the bowl hold long-stemmed water and red wine glasses. Chilled wine is held by the stem in such a way as not to warm the glass and, by extension, the wine. Tumblers are held near the base. Brandy snifters are cupped in the palm of the hand in order to warm the brandy.

Toasts: It is disrespectful for anyone NOT to participate in a toast. All who have notified the slave that they are non-drinkers will find their wine glasses have been filled with grape-juice for this ritual. When giving a Toast at a *formal* meal, everyone will STAND *unless* you are the person *receiving the toast* – in which case, you remain seated while everyone else stands. If this is an *informal* meal, everyone remains seated while the toast is offered.

- **Timing of the Toasts**: Once all food has been served, the most senior Head of Family who accepts that responsibility will offer a Toast.
- **Offering the Toast**: The person offering the Toast will raise his/her glass and offer the Toast. Once the Toast has been offered, everyone present will raise (but not touch) glasses.

"Beginning to Eat" **Protocols with slaves and submissives**: After food has been plated, but before any Family submissives may eat, Master takes a bite of food. At that signal, everyone at table – except the Family slaves/submissives – may begin to eat.

Next, Master will feed each Family slave and submissive a small forkful of food from his plate. **After** this ceremony, if the Alpha slave has a submissive in service, the Alpha slave will visibly signal this person when to eat. Once all the Family submissives have been provided a morsel, they may begin eating.

How to use your flatware – American Style – cutting food:

- **Fork** is held in the left hand, tines down, index finger on back of fork's stem pinning the food (such as a piece of meat).

- **Knife** is held in the right hand, index finger on back of knife blade. Cut one single piece of meat, use the knife if necessary to unpin the food from the fork, and then put the knife down onto the plate – blade facing toward the center of the plate. Unless you eat in the left-handed "European Style," transfer the fork to right hand – tines up – push the fork tines underneath, not into, the piece of food to pick it up. You may use your knife as a "pusher", if you need help getting foodstuffs onto your fork. Put the food in your mouth and replace the fork on plate, tines up, below your knife, which should be resting diagonally across the upper right rim of the plate.

- **Spoons**: The *dessert spoon* is longer than the *teaspoon* and is placed on the dessert plate at formal or informal meals. The *teaspoon* should appear in the saucer of the coffee cup, when served. The *soupspoon* is longer than the dessert spoon OR the teaspoon, and has an oval bowl. It is only used with crème soups. Remember to use a soup spoon by dipping it towards the back of the bowl, starting with the side of the spoon that's *away* from yourself, and pushing it towards the back of the bowl. This technique will help you keep your soup off of your clothes, because any drip will be more likely to travel forward underneath the spoon and land in your mouth than to fall directly off the bottom of the spoon. Try to avoid scraping the bottom of the soup bowl. When you are done with the spoon, place it on the soup plate to the right-hand side of the bowl.

Table Manners – General

Your mother was right: table manners DO count. Here is my version of a "critical list." Any slave/submissive in my service is expected at all times to follow these rules.

- Do not bring your cocktail glass to Table.

- Diners should have the same number of courses and start and finish at approximately the same time. That is, diners should monitor eating progress of their peers and speed up or slow down, as necessary. If my slave and I are dining alone, he/she is not to finish before me.

- Once you pick up a piece of cutlery, you should never put it back on the table. (Exception: if a "knife rest" has been provided, you may place your knife there between courses.)

- It is very impolite to season your food before you have tasted it. It is an insult to the Chef who prepared the meal and, thereby, it is also an insult to your host.

- Cut only enough food for the next mouthful.

- Do not speak with food in your mouth. Chew with your mouth closed and don't smack or crunch.

- Do not blow on hot liquids to cool them; stir them with a spoon and then test the temperature by taking a small spoonful of the liquid.

- Each Guest must take (and eat) a small portion from every serving dish. Nothing may be passed by.

- Do not "load up" your fork with food; dainty is good.

- If something is slightly out of reach at Table, ask that it be passed to you; do NOT start to rise out of your seat to reach for it, and do not reach in front of anyone else at the table to get something that you could have reached. Take the passed dish (or bread basket) from the person and thank them in a clear and deliberate voice. *Do not select an item from the dish (or basket) while the other guest is holding it.*

- Never lick your fingers after they have contacted food; your napkin is for that purpose.

- If you MUST remove something from your mouth (olive pit, piece of gristle) cover your mouth with your napkin, cup your other hand in front of your mouth to receive the rejected item. Place it as unobtrusively as you can upon your dinner plate.

- Never rub your lips with a napkin, pat them. Pat your mouth with your napkin before drinking from your wine or water glass to avoid leaving oils, grease or food particles on the rim of the glass.

- Soup spoons: For clear soups only: Do NOT place the entire spoon inside your mouth; sip the soup from the side of the spoon. (For cream soups, you may place the entire spoon in your mouth.)

- Leave the soupspoon IN the soup bowl, but do not leave the soupspoon in a bouillon cup or a cream soup bowl.

- Break bread and rolls in half with your fingers, then into single-bite pieces that you place in your mouth. Do NOT cut breads with a knife. Do NOT take a bite from the broken piece of bread or roll and place the remainder back onto the bread plate.

- If butter and/or jam are served, after transferring a small portion from the serving dish to your bread plate, spread the butter on individual bites of bread, not on the entire side of the bread or roll.

- Jams and condiments go onto the bread plate first, not directly onto the bread.

- Keep arms and elbows OFF the table in the US (until you have completed each course, at which point it is generally considered acceptable to lean on the table in order to hear conversations better). On the European Continent, it is customary to rest your forearm ON the table, so that your hands are in clear view. The exception in the US is that between courses, you may momentarily rest your forearms on the table, so long as you do not turn your back on your partner.

- Don't slump at the table. Sit forward in your chair, showing your interest in the conversation.

- Avoid curling your feet around the chair legs; similarly, avoid stretching your feet out under the table.

- When you finish your meal, DON'T push your plate back. Leave it alone.

- The slave(s) will remove any crumbs that have fallen onto the table. Don't touch anything that has fallen onto the table surface.

- Place your napkin in your chair when leaving the Table temporarily, otherwise, place the napkin to the right of the place setting at the end of the meal when leaving the table; NEVER place your napkin on a used plate.

Table Manners – Restaurant Dining

These additional Rules are provided for the slave when dining outside the home. While these Rules are written as though Master is serving as Host, they apply equally if another person is hosting the meal.

- Without asking specific permission, the slave will not order a main course that takes longer to prepare than the main course that Master orders.

- The slave will not request that Master order a meal that is more expensive than Master's meal, *unless* Master specifically recommends a meal to you that is pricey.

- Order food that is easy to eat, not too messy. This is particularly relevant if Master is entertaining Others at a restaurant. For example, it's often difficult to look bright and witty (or humble and submissive), if you're fighting with your angel-hair pasta.

- As previously mentioned, taste first, season second. In this setting, Others will notice if you season your food without first tasting it. In the world of business, this suggests that you reach conclusions without assessing the facts.

- If you do not like the food or the way it was prepared, keep this information to yourself, unless a food-safety issue is involved. Master *does not* like food discussed at the table.

We are dining out to have a good time, not to discuss the meal, other than in very general and complimentary terms.

- Foods you can touch with your fingers include:
  o artichoke
  o asparagus (may be eaten with the fingers, as long as it is not covered with sauce or otherwise prepared so it is too mushy to pick up easily)
  o bread
  o chips, French fries, fried chicken and hamburgers
  o corn on the cob
  o cookies
  o crisp bacon (but not limp bacon)
  o hors d'oeuvres, canapés, crudités (anything served at a cocktail party)
  o olives, celery and pickles
  o sandwiches that are not open-faced, not too tall to fit in the mouth, not saturated with dripping sauces or loaded with mushy fillings; that is, sandwiches that are intended to be picked up and eaten – otherwise use your fork and knife
  o small fruits and berries on the stem, most often, fresh strawberries with the hulls attached

Monitoring Guests During the Meal

The slave will closely monitor water and wine glasses and guests' plates. From time to time, the slave will arise from Table and re-fill water and wine glasses for all guests and for Master/Mistress. If a guest appears to be a hearty diner and has completed his or her serving, the slave will arise and offer a second helping for that Guest or for Master.

Changing Courses Protocols

When multiple courses are involved, the slave(s) will do two things: first, use a crumber to remove any food or crumbs that have fallen onto the table surface; second, clear away the plate belonging to the prior course and bring the prepared plate for the ensuing course. [Note: Protocols for changing plates for a multi-course meal have already been presented.]

Dinner Ending Protocols
Finishing a Meal: The slave will take extreme care *never* to end a meal before Master.

Getting the Signal: Master will signal the end of dinner and escort the appropriate person to the living room. "Appropriate person," previously described, would be my own slave (if this is a *Dining In*) or the most senior person at Table (if this is a *Dining Out*).

Getting Up from Table: At a formal dinner, slaves and submissives will rise as they see their Masters (or Doms) rise.

Proceeding to Living Room: Guests will be escorted to the living room. The slave will ask each guest for his/her preference of liqueurs and selections will be brought out on serving tray. After liqueurs have been served, slave(s) will proceed to clear the table.

Table Clearing Protocol: The slave is not to stack the china plates when removing them from the table. Carry one plate per hand per trip. Remove dishes to the kitchen and soak them in the rubber tub that fits inside the sink. Take care to be as quiet as possible.

Cleanup Immediately After Company Leaves

Dining Room
Entirely clear the table. Remove all the table linen and place it in the laundry room to be dealt with later. Clean and then remove/store the table's silence pad (if used).

Clean the table. If it is a wooden table, clean with Pledge®; if it is a glass table, clean with Windex®.

Reset the table with a formal setting for three people. To summarize: in one stack, stack the plates as follows: charger plate; dinner plate; salad plate. Flatware as follows: knife and teaspoon to the right of the stack of plates, salad and dinner forks to the left of the stack of plates. Our Family protocol calls for a diagonal placement of the water and wine glasses, as described above. The name card holders are centered two inches above the top of the plates. In our Family, the cards for Master, Mistress and my slave are always set. Master is positioned to the right of Mistress, my slave to my right (thus, I'm in the middle). Replace the candles and flowers. Be sure there is no wax upon the candleholder. If candleholder is silver, verify that it is polished. Replace the salt and pepper shakers and the wine caddy.

Kitchen

Dishes: Hand wash everything; do not use dishwasher – too harsh on the china and silver. Use the dishwasher as a drying rack. Use Dawn® kitchen soap. Use rubber gloves.

Stemware: hand wash using lukewarm water, rinse well under running water. To obtain extra sparkle; hold the glasses over some steaming water for 30 seconds. Use a lint-free linen towel without any fabric softener to dry stem and glassware. Hold the glass by the bowl, not the stem, which is fragile, and gently polish off the water. Don't force the towel into the bowl as the glass is thin and might break. Just leave the glass turned upside down and let it drain itself onto a towel.

Hand dry the following: Stemware, crystal, and bone china.

Scour the kitchen sink and related counters. Use Cameo® to scour a stainless steel kitchen sink; use Barkeeper's Friend® for a porcelain sink. Also use Barkeeper's Friend® to clean all kitchen counter sur-faces. Use 409® to clean the stovetop and stove vent. Use a "bar rag" or equivalent to dry the sink and counters after cleaning.

Chapter 6

The slave's Job as Personal Assistant

Maid Services

House Care – Cleanup, Day after Entertaining

Process the linen napkins; wash them by hand. Either iron the napkins after they have dried or dry them by wringing them out and stretching them flat on the clean kitchen counter, taking care to remove all air bubbles (this is a natural way of creating a napkin that will look as though it has been ironed).

Fold the napkins per House Protocol and place the necessary number on the top service plate. Extra napkins go in the linen closet.

Vacuum all living room and dining room carpets. Use Endust® when dusting. Use Liquid Gold® or Pledge® on kitchen chairs and on all wood furniture. Verify that all surfaces are neat and tidy; all books and magazines put away; play toys sanitized and replaced.

Mop all tile floors. Use Mr. Clean® (orange scented) detergent. "Load" the mop in this solution. Mop a section of floor, rinse the mop under tap water, NOT back in the detergent solution, then re-load the mop in detergent solution and continue mopping.

Fully clean all bathrooms. Clean commode and sink and mop the floors. Fold the last sheet of toilet paper to a point to signal that the room has been cleaned. If necessary, wash the throw rug(s). Clean all counters, leaving *nothing* on them. Clean all mirrors with Windex®.

House Care – General Standing Orders
Level One Cleaning

Vacuum heavily used areas, particularly in the Master bath and closet and in the Master bedroom.

Ensure all surfaces are neat and tidy, nothing out of place. In the Master bath, be sure that the towels are cleaned, if necessary, and that they are hung up correctly. Polish the chrome water faucets on the vanity, in the bath and in the shower. Be sure that the counter surfaces are "sponged."

In the Master bedroom, make the bed and change sheets, if needed. Be sure that all surfaces are dusted, if needed. Be sure that nothing that can be put away is left out.

In the kitchen, spray all stovetop and counter surfaces with 409® and wipe them clean. Put away all dishes. Polish the chrome faucets and either wipe out or scour the sink, depending upon its condition.

Our Family Protocol calls for both the dining room and informal kitchen tables to be set – do that after the kitchen is cleaned.

Attend to the playroom or other rooms in the house, as needed (little, if anything, should be needed).

Do load(s) of laundry and iron, as needed. Empty all the house trash-cans.

Level Two Cleaning – as above, plus...

Use cleanser (Bartenders Friend®, not Ajax®) on all Formica surfaces. Use cleansers on all sinks in all bathrooms and the kitchen. Clean the tile around the shower door. Use 409® on stove vent area and on stove back-splashes. Vacuum the remainder of the house.

Clean ashes out of fireplace; sweep hearth. Seasonally, ensure adequate firewood is on clean hearth. Sweep and mop kitchen floor; check all woodwork around light switches and door handles for smudge marks; remove same.

Run an empty load through the dishwasher and ensure that it is spotless, inside and out.

Clean all windowsills.

Level Three Cleaning: As above, plus...
Dust the house, including picture frames, wooden bowls and furniture surfaces. Scour the shower/bathtub(s).

Vacuum all floors that need also to be mopped. Mop all floors, including bathroom floors. Wash all bathroom rugs and clean all mirror surfaces.

Remove everything from refrigerator and clean all surfaces. Clean top of refrigerator, washer and dryer; clean inside microwave and inside oven.

Lift out and clean all stove burners; lift the entire stove surface and clean below the elements. Replace any aluminum "protectors" that fit immediately below the heating elements.

Check AC filters – and change if necessary.

Level Four Cleaning: As above, plus
Clean all baseboards and woodwork; clean all windows, inside only. Clean all ceiling fan blades. Clean the freezer.

Valet Services

Preparing New Boots
The slave will follow these Protocols for *new boots* that aren't oil tanned. The purpose is to get the new boots to shine and keep them shining with ease.

Beware: new boots are not easy to work with. Most new boots have a coating on them that will keep them looking new for many years. This coating must come off in order to get the polish to stick. Not all boots are equal, the more they cost, the more coating they will have on them.

Supplies:

- Rubbing alcohol
- Scrub sponges
- Soft cloth – preferably cheesecloth

Actions to take:

1) In a small bowl, soak a sponge in a solution of equal parts of water and alcohol.

2) Use the sponge to rub the boot lightly in small circles to take off the coating mentioned above. (WARNING: This can be tricky. The slave must be very careful not to scratch the leather; scratched leather will require additional work.)

   The slave will notice that as the sponge is repeatedly dipped in the water/alcohol mix, it starts looking milky. That means that the slave is successfully removing the undesired coating. If the mix becomes too milky, change it for a fresh mix. Keep at it; this can take some time. Beware: it is difficult to determine when all the coating has been removed. When it looks as though the boot leather is wet, you are almost there. Once the leather starts to get wet you must be very careful to change to a soft cloth so that you do not scratch the leather.

3) To test if the coating is off, let the leather of the boot dry **NATURALLY**. **NEVER** put polish on wet leather; the leather will mold. Don't try to hurry the drying process by putting it in the oven at a really low heat. There is a substantial risk of damaging the boots. Once the leather is dry, apply a small amount of polish to the tip of the boot to make sure it soaks in and polishes to a shine.

   Now, put the boots on and walk a few steps. If the coating is **not** off, the polish you just added will crack – sometimes the polish will just fall off. If you do not initially see any cracks, walk some more to make sure.

4) If you **DO** see some cracks, repeat step two and continue until there are no cracks.

5) These steps are the same if the slave ever has to strip boots down.

6) Once boots are thoroughly dry, proceed to the next step, polishing them.

Polishing Boots

After each use, boots will **always** be shined according to this Protocol.

Supplies:

- Saddle soap
- Rag
- Clean cloth, 100% cotton – preferably cheesecloth
- Soft Polish brush
- Small bowl of water
- Black boot polish

Actions to take:

1) Make sure the boots are clean: Master does not want the slave to polish in any dirt. The slave will use saddle soap to clean the boots. Saddle soap will foam. This foam helps to remove the dirt from the leather (making it easy to get off). Now, using a damp rag, remove all the saddle soap and let the boots dry thoroughly.

2) Before proceeding, the slave will wash hands with soap and water, as body oil – and oils in general – will inhibit formation of the shine.

3) Next, the slave will put a small amount of polish on his/her fingers (applying polish with fingers puts the slave more in touch with the process). Using small circular motions, apply polish to the boots until they are covered. Use a brush to bring out the polish in the boots.

4) For a high shine, add polish to clean cheesecloth, then lightly dip it in water and polish the area. As the end approaches, the slave will notice that the cloth will glide increasingly easily over the polished area. As a variant,

add saliva to the polish on the cloth. Some Masters may wish that the polish is applied by the slave's tongue. [Note #1: For this shine, the slave must NOT use a brush, as this will leave streaks in the polish. Note #2: If the slave applies the polish by tongue, Lincoln Polish is rumored to have a better taste than Kiwi®. Officer Wes points out that this is odd, because Kiwi® is a Sara Lee brand and Lincoln Polish® is a Sara Lee product.]

Extra Care for Boots

The slave is directed to attend to certain details of this ritual, as Leatherfolk will notice the little things that are *not done,* such as the boot's eyelet, sole and even the boot's tongue.

1) Use a permanent marker to blacken the eyelets. The slave will be very careful not to let the marker touch the leather.

2) Use a toothbrush to get into the hard-to-get to places, such as where the sole meets the leather of the boot. This spot is really hard to reach, so use a little polish on the brush.

3) The slave will use a black candle to cover severe scratches in the boot. Caution: the candle must be black all the way through (not just a top layer of black coloring on a white or clear candle). Let some candle wax pool, then drip the wax onto the scratch – smooth the boot surface.

4) The slave will use edge dressing on the side of the boot soles. Again, be careful not to get any of the dressing on the leather. Edge dressing is **paint**, and it is bad for leather.

Note: Kiwi® makes a Heel and Sole Edge Color Renew. It is sold in an applicator bottle. Be careful not to get it on any other surface. The slave will work on a surface well protected with newspaper – which is where the boots belong while they are drying.

When the edge dressing is finished, the slave will rinse off the applicator brush and dry it before putting it away. The applicator will last longer this way.

General Tips:

- Never use any kind of "instant shine" spray. It is just *spray paint* and it cannot be removed from the leather. It will dye the leather – and then, you've got a major problem.

- Do NOT use any type of "easy care" products; they are not good for the leather.

- If the slave takes boots to the shoe store to be re-dyed, be sure to tell them NOT to put a top coat on the leather.

- Do NOT EVER put a water resistant spray on leather. Instead, use a product such as Dubbin®. This will protect the leather and will make it water resistant.

- If boots start to develop a foul odor, sprinkle some baking soda in them and leave it there overnight.

Care of Leather Clothing

This protocol instructs the slave in ways of taking care of softer leather items such as vests, pants, jackets and gloves. The slave will inspect all my leather clothing after each use and use good judgment to determine whether or not any piece needs care.

1) Never work on wet leather. To avoid causing creases or cracking, always lay these items flat or on a hanger to dry. Always be careful to keep my leather out of the sun.

2) Examine the leather. If the slave finds any portion that is fading, use a soft shoe polish to bring back the color. The softer the polish, the better it will soak into the leather. It will take an hour or two for the leather to soak up all the polish into its pores.

3) Leather cream or Dubbin® can be applied directly on top of polish. Dubbin® will really bring out the leather's luster. If the leather quickly soaks up the Dubbin®, the slave will add another coat the next day, after the leather has had ample time to soak up the first application.

Tips:
If the slave finds that some of my leather has developed mildew, report it to me immediately, and we will discuss how the slave let this happen, and how amends will be made.

By way of remedy, the slave will take one cup of water and one cup of rubbing alcohol on a sponge and work the affected area. Let it dry completely, and then use saddle soap to clean the area. Polish and add Dubbin®.

For salt stains, use 1 cup hot water and 1 tablespoon of white vinegar and rub on affected area let dry, clean, polish and condition.

Equipment Care
Clean floggers by sponging (not soaking) with a solution of warm water to which 5% dishwashing liquid has been added. Be sure to dry the leather thoroughly by squeezing and blotting the falls with paper towels. Do not use any artificial form of heat. Leather does not like to get wet and will remain stiff if not dried adequately.

If the floggers need to be decontaminated, use an ample supply of 70% Isopropyl alcohol, scrubbing with a soft brush if body fluids need to be removed. Spin the whip to aid in the natural process of evaporation/drying.

After cleaning and decontaminating the flogger, restore the natural oils to the falls by using "leather dressings" such as Dubbin®, Lexol® or Pecards®. For floggers other than black, be sure to use a neutral color product. Also, be sure the flogger is dry before applying a small amount of the dressing. The slave will work this dressing into the falls with bare hands, allowing a couple of hours for absorption; wipe off any excess with a soft cloth. Allow the flogger to hang after this treatment.

For insertables, after every use, wash in 90% Isopropyl alcohol. Put all cleaned toys away where they belong. Wash all sheets and towels used in play using bleach, if necessary.

Personal Care of Master
Bathing Preparations
Keep track of number of times razor blade has been used. Replace blade after five uses.

Ensure that bath or shower is prepared with:
- Razor designated for shaving Master's head
- Antibacterial shaving cream
- Bar of aromatic soap – preferably musk or sandalwood scents

Inside the bathroom, in general, preparations include ensuring:
- Bathroom candles are lit (after trimming, if necessary)
- Scene music is playing
- Overhead lights have been dimmed, as appropriate

Showering
Place bathmat outside shower area and stand by to dry Master upon emerging from shower. After Master has been dried, wipe down the shower stall and replace the bathmat.

Taking a Bath
Light candles in bathtub areas, remembering to trim the wicks, if necessary. Draw bath water to temperature of 104 degrees (using meat thermometer to verify). Ask Master which bath salts, etc, he wishes added; add same. Place bath mat beside bathtub and place towels within easy reach of bathtub. Have wine or cocktail prepared and positioned by bathtub. Enter the bath and wash Master, as directed. During the bath, raise the water temperature to 106 degrees and make sure that temperature is maintained by adding hot water. After bath, dry him with the warmed towel. Clean the bathtub with cleanser and remove all accoutrements (glasses, etc.) from the area.

Dressing
Master will direct the slave to organize specific clothing required for the day or evening. The slave will set this clothing out, along with underwear/socks and shoes, as is customary. The slave will assist Master in dressing, including zipping/buttoning pants and shirt.

Preparing the Bedroom at Night
There are two bedtime protocols for the slave. The first is to turn down the comforter and sheets on Master's side of the bed; second is to "smudge" the room with Native American sage-bundles prepared for that purpose.

The protocol for smudging the room is to close the bedroom door, to light the smudge bundle and to walk around the room smudging the outside perimeter. (Note: slave is to take care not to over-smudge the room. If it becomes "over-smudged", the slave is to air it out some. The room should have a faint lingering scent of sage.)

Driving and Car Maintenance
In certain instances, the slave will serve as Master's chauffeur. This will include proper dress as a chauffeur, including cap and blazer. The slave will also be responsible for the vehicle. The slave will ensure proper vehicle maintenance, including monitoring the need for oil changes and having them done every 3,000 miles. The slave will keep the car's interior spotless and the car floors vacuumed. The slave will also keep the car washed on a regular basis.

Shopping
The slave will keep the shopping list updated. When any item is used up, it must be listed. Heavily used items should have back-up quantities stored (applesauce, plastic wrap...). When re-purchasing heavily used items, purchase more than one, so we have backups in the house.

Meats: The slave will take care to purchase high-quality meats, attending to the grade of the meat (prime beef preferred) and the amount of marbling.

Fruits and vegetables: Master prefers that certain items *always* be available in the house – including: apples, mushrooms, black seedless grapes, celery, bananas, parsley, and salad fixings. Items such as asparagus, parsley and celery must be stored in water in the refrigerator.

Chef Services

The slave is expected to become a gourmet cook. It is expected that the slave will become particularly adept at the art of *presenting* food on a plate and on a table. This slave is expected to identify relevant courses of study, nationally or internationally.

Kitchen Management

At Master's expense, the slave is expected to purchase and maintain cooking pots, pans, utensils and equipment needed to fulfill this Task. This includes subscribing to specialty publications and catalogs and purchasing requisite cookbooks.

The slave is expected to know and to follow correct procedures for storing wines. This extends to organizing our wines and turning them while in storage.

Food Pairing Preferences

While this section has to be modified for your own tastes, over the years, I have developed tastes for certain condiments with certain foods. That list – an Instruction to my own slave – is as follows:

Food	Condiment
Pork	Applesauce
Lamb	Mint jelly
Prime Rib	Spiced peach; spiced mango
Pot Roast	Apple sauce, potato pancakes
Turkey, chicken	Cranberry sauce

Note: When you write your own Manual of Protocol, you may choose to expand this section to suit your own preferences.

Storing and Packaging Foods

The slave will wrap foods in Saran® wrap, use only Saran® wrap, not a competitor – Master is concerned about plasticizers in certain brands of cling wrap) or place them in the appropriate sized plastic storage container before placing them in the refrigerator. That is, if food has been brought back from a restaurant, or if food is left over from a meal, it is to be stored in such a way as to maximize the storage life and minimize air contact. At no time is a "take-home" box to be placed in the refrigerator; the food that has been brought home is to be individually wrapped and stored.

Executive Secretary Services

The slave is Master's representative in many domains, not the least when answering the phone for Master.

Telephone Protocols
Answering the telephone
The slave is Master's representative. Treat this role seriously. Endeavor to answer the phone by the third ring. Always answer the phone by standing (or when standing). Before speaking, SMILE. Use a friendly voice; speak slowly and enunciate clearly.

Say: "Good morning." (or "Good afternoon." or "Good evening.") "This is XXXXX's home, how may I assist you?"

Conversation options
The slave recognizes the caller and knows that Master wishes to take the call: "Yes Ma'am. (or, "Yes, Sir.") I'll get Master."

The slave recognizes the caller, but is not sure that Master wishes to take the call: "Sir (or "Ma'am") I'll need to see whether Master can take this call right now."

The slave doesn't recognize the caller: "Ma'am, (or "Sir,") this is XXXXX's assistant, may I help you?

The slave recognizes the caller and KNOWS that Master doesn't wish to have this conversation at this time: "Sir," (or "Ma'am,") Master is deeply involved in a project right now and has left Instructions not to be disturbed. May I take a message?"

Taking messages
A formal message pad will be found by the bed in the Master bedroom and on Master's desk, under the telephone. Pens will be with each

message pad. In the kitchen, the message pad is in the same drawer as the scissors.

If the slave can't get to the formal message pad, the slave MUST transfer the message to a pad so that the note left will stand out from other scraps of paper.

The message should include: the person's full name (unless the slave knows that Master knows this person – if there is the *slightest doubt* take down the name). VERIFY LAST NAME SPELLING. The telephone number (verify that the call is local or obtain the area code.) Read the number back to the caller to verify its accuracy. Record the subject of the call (don't be shy in asking; the slave is Master's representative and speaks with Master's authority).

The message MUST be placed on Master's desk – preferably on the computer keyboard (subtlety won't work in this case).

Preparing Letters
General comment: Master generally prepares his own letters. If the slave is asked to prepare a letter, it will NOT be sent until Master has read it for tone and content.

Font, font size, margins
- Margins: 1.2" all the way around
- Font style: Arial
- Font size: 11 point on 13 pica leading

Style comments: The tone of the letter will be formal, but conversational. The letter should sound as though you're *speaking* with the other person. Be concise; don't be chatty.

Preparing Briefing Memos for Master
Master requires a specific format for *one page* "briefing memos." My slave will follow this format:
- **Background** (what led up to this memo)
- **Facts** (be careful to keep *opinion* out of this section)
- **Alternatives** (the first alternative is always: "Do nothing")
- **Recommendation** (with justification)

Maintain Insurance

Our basic house insurance includes: fire, casualty, umbrella liability and contents insurance. There is a rider on this policy covering specific listed items. The slave will become familiar with this policy and discuss any questions with Master. It is the slave's responsibility to ensure that substantial new purchases are added to the insurance rider for this policy.

Auto, health and dental insurance: review annually to ensure relevant coverage.

An Evening Out

The slave will ask Master for direction on the general type of evening to be planned. If it is a dinner, the slave will inquire as to the type of food, level of service and price range that Master intends. The slave will also ask about the kind of entertainment sought, if any. This could include theater, cinema, music, dance, or other.

The slave will conduct relevant research and inform Master of the key options (best 2-3 choices) and, upon Instruction, the slave will make relevant reservations.

Planning for Trips

Please refer to Appendix C for an example of our "pre-trip checklist."

Making reservations: Master recommends using Priceline (www. Priceline.com) or similar hotel search engine for reservations. Master prefers a four-star hotel.

On-site Logistics: After reservations have been made, call that hotel's *Concierge* and ask: What are the "don't miss" places in the city and "What special and romantic" restaurants can he/she recommend? Master likes really interesting places. High-visual stimulations. Interesting foods. Conduct necessary Internet searches for that city/ location. In particular, do Google and Yahoo searches for photo sites that may highlight that area.

Air Flights: For Southwest Air, via internet: http://www.southwest.com; for other air reservations use my CitiTravel membership. See me for access codes.

Prepare "Munchies" for trip. This includes: raisins, dates, nuts, candy bars, power bars etc.

Prepare a folder containing all key information, such as maps and *detailed* directions to the hotel and/or activities we will be attending. If we're driving, any places to stop along the way that are *interesting*. All relevant hotel, car rental and airline contact and confirmation numbers must be in this folder. CRITICAL: the "weather report sheet" must be in the folder, too.

Ensure that I have obtained adequate cash/travelers checks: verify balances on all credit cards that we're taking along.

Courtesan Services

While this section may be somewhat more relevant for a female slave, many of these issues and themes are – in fact – right on point for a male slave.

The tradition of the "Courtesan" comes from ancient Greece and Rome. It reappeared in 14th century Renaissance Italy, was later brought to the French Court and continued as a tradition in post-Revolutionary France until the late 1800s. Courtesans, women serving the Royal Court, were schooled in the finest and best of the Female Arts. Courtesans glided, they did not walk. They always knew *le mot juste* for any situation. They spoke elegantly, dressed elegantly, walked elegantly, were excellent hostesses, accomplished lovers, brilliant conversationalists, exhibited great wit and charm and were extraordinarily seductive. Many were excellent writers, musicians, artists and dancers. These skills are similar to what one might expect of a Geisha – the way she dresses, wears her hair and makeup, the way she walks, moves, talks, entertains and converses. It's the *Total Package*.

In this country, short of having grown up among the social aristocracy, having been groomed for a socially prominent marriage and having attended some type of charm school or finishing school, these kinds of personal behaviors in a woman are extremely rare. Thus, an adult female slave may need quite a bit of exposure to new educational experiences and a huge dose of self-focus and concentration to master Courtesan or Geisha skills. It also takes an Owner who is interested in investing the considerable time, money and effort to form his slave into this sort of art piece.

Personal Appearance and Behavior
Speaking/Gesturing

The slave will be sensitive to the difference between the connotations of words. Word connotation affects both the tone and temper of a person's projected being. For example, in English, one "speaks with" or one "talks to." As one "talks to" a subordinate, this form of oral communication is closed to my slave when communicating with me. The slave may or may not elect to talk to his/her family members, as that is not my concern. This point concerns *tone* and *attitude.* It also concerns *unconscious communication* with Others. That is, there is risk in mindless talking, as opposed to purposeful speaking. As *mindfulness in all things* is a key concept for the Courtesan, these points are relevant.

When speaking, the slave will modulate his/her voice to be as pleasant as possible, never loud, bossy or overbearing. The slave will avoid using a high vocal pitch, a nasal inflection, chattering, mumbling or whining, and will speak slowly and with a strong voice in order to command attention and respect – while being appropriately deferential.

The slave will avoid using excessive arm or hand movements, as these can be distracting to others and detract from the discussion. The slave will also be as lucid and eloquent as possible, using the fewest and most effective words to convey thoughts. This is where a large vocabulary (previously discussed) comes into play. The slave will always be aware of the effect of words on others (direct meaning as well as connotation) and be keenly aware of when to change the subject or when to stop speaking altogether.

Many times there will be non-verbal clues from listeners reflecting their conversational comfort level. While the slave should be sensitive to these cues, the slave should not feel as though he/she needs to carry the conversation alone. The most effective method is to get Others to speak about themselves – remember: "It's more important to be interested than interesting." But, even with that basic understanding, members of this Family are to keep abreast of current events as much as possible in order to have *Something to Say* in social settings.

Walking
The slave will walk in a graceful manner at all times without making undue noise or drawing undue attention. The slave will take light steps and will not bounce; the slave will glide as though balancing a book on his/her head. Legs should be kept close together with one foot placed in front of the other. Arms should move from the elbows, not from the shoulder.

Entering and Exiting Vehicles
The proper way to enter a vehicle is first to sit on the car seat facing outwards with legs together, then rotate the body into the car *as a unit* to end up facing forward. When exiting, reverse the process. The slave will rise to a standing position using the legs, not the upper body.

Entering and exiting *trucks* poses more of a challenge since the use of a running board is usually required to enter the cab of the pickup. The slave will always wait for Master to open the car door for the slave, unless instructed otherwise.

Sitting
Sitting at Table: When sitting at Table, the slave will be seated in an upright position, legs together. The slave will not slouch or place elbows on the table during the meal. Hands are usually kept in the lap when not eating. When being seated, the slave will always enter from the left, arise from the right. Particularly for female slaves, the slave will lower herself to the edge of the chair and then center her torso on the seat surface, adjusting the chair position forward or back as necessary. Legs are kept together with feet crossed at the ankles. (Note: As previously covered, it is our protocol that the slave is always

seated by Master at Table. However, after being seated initially (and after the "centering" ceremony, the slave will have to rise to serve the meal and, throughout the meal, may have to rise to refill water or wine glasses.)

Sitting other than at Table: Here, the slave is responsible for exhibiting grace and elegance in motion. If the slave is female, she expected to exude "ladylike demeanor."

For the Female slave

Makeup/hair/nails: Makeup should never be garish or applied in a heavy manner, unless it's for a certain reason, such as an appearance at a fetish party, or for a photographic session where heavier makeup may be called for. Colors used should be appropriate for the color and skin type of the slave. Hair should be washed frequently and kept neatly coiffed in a style that pleases Master. Coloring may be used at Master's discretion. Nails should be manicured on a regular basis. Use of professionally-applied acrylics is permitted, but not required. Use of colored polish on the nails is also permitted.

Dress/clothing/perfume: Evening Dress has already been covered; day dress shall generally be all black (Master also tends to wear black during the day). Perfume should be used in moderation; do not overwhelm Master with scent. Master loves Women, not necessarily *perfume.*

Host/Hostess Skills

The slave is expected to serve as Master's Host or Hostess. The slave is expected to make the guests feel as welcomed as possible and attempt to anticipate their needs in advance. Some guests may have special needs, such as dietary restrictions or health issues that may have to be addressed by tailoring food selections to their requirements. For those who visit often, it is always a sign of extreme respect to have their favorite items on hand for their use. The slave shall keep a 3-ring binder listing special guest needs, and alphabetized by the guest's name, better to ensure advanced preparation for subsequent visits. This listing will include items such as physical or dietary needs. These are also butler skills.

Entertainment

The slave is expected to entertain Master. The slave is expected to have or to develop musical and/or voice skills and to improve them over time in order to bring pleasure to Master. To reinforce the importance of this skill, Master will make time available for his slave to take music and/or voice lessons and to maintain skill through appropriate practice.

In addition to musical skills, the slave is expected to be able to dance and to learn different styles of dance in order to please Master and to serve him as a dance partner. Master will arrange necessary dance lessons.

Artistic and Literary Pursuits

The slave is expected to have skills in the arts. The slave is expected to be skilled in areas such as oral recitation, writing, speaking, painting, photography, flower arranging, calligraphy, needlework or other areas of Master's interest. This furthers the slave's personal growth and brings delight to Master when his slave is personally fulfilled. Classes in any of these areas are greatly encouraged. Additionally, the slave is expected to assist Master in researching and writing whenever requested.

Indoor/Outdoor Recreational Activities

The slave is expected to participate in outdoor activities. Though this might not typically be considered to fall within the category of Courtesan or Geisha skills, in this day and age, it's important that the slave be well-rounded and flexible in order to participate in a wide range of social situations. The occasion may arise when Master wishes the slave participate in some activity such as baseball, basketball, biking, camping, fishing, hiking, horseback riding, ice skating, playing pool, playing cards and board games, roller skating, cross-country snow skiing, water sports, swimming, tennis, volleyball, croquet, or shuffleboard and the like. Not only must the slave be physically prepared for these activities, but should know enough about them to be able to participate.

Sexual Techniques
The slave is expected to be thoroughly knowledgeable (and widely read) in the art of lovemaking. Master expects the slave to be creative and inventive in this area.

Healing Arts
The slave is expected to expand upon existing gifts in the healing arts. This includes continuing to learn and to master specialty areas such as Reiki, hypnosis and other alternative healing techniques and practices. The slave is expected to use these gifts for the benefit of Master and Others.

Epilogue

Some Thoughts for Readers

Live in the Present

Recently, a woman was being interviewed on National Public Radio after her husband died. With an obvious tremor in her voice, she commented that: "The five months since he died have been longer than the 58 years we were married."

This grabbed me. I realized just how important my relationship with my slave has become, how important my slave is to me. Every evening is *special* because we both work hard to make it so. I hope that this book has given you some ideas to adapt to your own lives and loves.

Many Try It, Few Succeed

Unfortunately, M/s relationships are known for their brevity. They seldom last. If you look at those few that DO last, the couples are generally very mature (in age) and have been married a time or two. They know what worked and what didn't work in "vanilla" relationships, and they've been through enough personal self-examination (with or without a therapist) to know how to work with (manage?) their partner over the long term.

In important ways, the fantasy of a Master/slave relationship differs from the reality of it. Conducting a Master/slave play scene differs from the reality of living 24/7 in the M/s culture. From the Master's viewpoint, it takes work to feed the emotional needs of the person serving as the slave. And the Master must appreciate that every act of obedience, every act of service, is a gift to him from his slave. What does Master offer that earns this kind of Gift, this kind of Honor,

Respect and Devotion? The Master has to appreciate why it would be that someone would make this bargain with him.

Step back, for a moment, from what you've been reading in this book. Consider, for a moment, that every bit of it is real. My slave is serving as my valet, butler, chef, secretary, hostess, entertainer, research assistant, nurse, healer, maid, kinky play partner, and sex partner extraordinaire. This is a full-time job. The added responsibility of caring for the slave's biological family in a vanilla setting means that my slave is working overtime. It takes tremendous commitment on everyone's part to keep these worlds separate.

So, both Master and slave have to be really, really clear about the goal, the Purpose of this kind of *structured relationship*. Both adults must be psychologically stable and be working in unison to support life within the M/s dynamic.

Considering the slave for a moment, there's a vast difference from *thinking* you would like to be a slave and *having a slaveheart*. Unless this relationship structure grabs your heart AND your mind, it's not likely to work very long. But, this is something each of you has to find out on your own. If you haven't already done so, I recommend reading Guy Baldwin's book <u>Slavecraft</u>. Read it slowly and read it more than once. Also, read Guy Baldwin's <u>Ties that Bind</u>. Then, start attending the regional and national Master/slave conferences (there are five regional feeder conferences and one International M/s conference at this writing – Appendix F). Read extensively on the few *real* Leather websites you can find. If you are lucky enough to live near a chapter of MAsT (Masters and slaves Together), join it.

Leathersex: The Goal of it All.

The *spiritual dynamic* is, in my opinion, one of the defining differences between *Leather* and *Not-Leather*. As Guy Baldwin puts it: "When leather and SM scenes were done in a certain way, we achieved a different level of awareness – we felt transformed into someone whom it felt better to be. Also, a kind of bonding occurred between SM players that had been missing in our more usual sexual encounters" (*Ties that Bind* p. 34). What I will add here, is that after sufficient practice at sexual play techniques, it is not uncommon for my sexual partner to go into subspace from these activities alone – absent any SM. I live for the surprise they later express at this. This is called "sex magic", and although it's whispered about, it's hard to find much written about it. You may start with <u>Sensuous Magic</u> by Pat Califia and <u>Secrets of Western Sex Magic</u> by Frater U∴D∴. Of these two, the latter is more on-point.

And That's a Wrap

I hope you've enjoyed this book. It's a window into another culture. Some readers will appreciate the view; others are likely to condemn me for having written it. At its core, this is an etiquette book with an attitude. Readers should feel free to write to me with questions: Robert@RubelPresents.com In the subject line, please put the phrase: **book contact** (I have a strong spam filter and that phrase automatically grabs your e-mail and keeps it from being flung out into the emptiness of cyberspace.

An M/s Studies Book

Appendices

Appendix A
Example of Training Contract

[Note: this is in a form that I have actually used.
Still, you would have to modify it for your particular circumstances.]

Dated: _____

Preamble
This Contract is between_____, hereinafter referred to as Master, and _____, hereinafter referred to as *the slave*.

(Because this contract was initially developed for a *third* in our Family, this next line was included in this actual Contract: *This Contract is offered directly between _____ and _____ and lives outside the Leather Family structure to which _____ is party.*)

Caveat
This contract is not legally binding, and is meant only as an aid to better understand the needs, duties and responsibilities of _____ and _____ as they begin a period of slave training.

Commitment and Termination
I, _____, hereinafter referred to as *the slave*, do of my own free will, and being of sound mind and body, hereby offer myself in consensual training to _____ _____, hereinafter referred to as Master, for the period beginning _____ and ending on _____, unless extended or terminated in writing at a different date.

Either party may terminate this Contract at any time before the above named date only in the event of a material breach. Prior to _____ _____, this Contract will be reviewed, renegotiated and rewritten, or terminated.

Mutual Respect

This contract describes the respective roles and responsibilities of Master and slave. This contract assumes that each party holds the other in equal respect; that Master and slave each think of the other as having equal value to themselves. Master is not *better* than the slave; the slave is not *less than* the Master.

Contract Provisions

1. To the best of this slave's ability, this slave pledges to honor the terms and the spirit of this Contract and to study to develop the skills and knowledge necessary to serve Master's wishes and desires. This service will be without ego, pride or expectations. From this day until the termination or extension of this Contract, this slave pledges at all times to obey Master with humility and to subvert the slave's will and desires to his will and desires. To the extent possible, this slave will hide nothing from Master and answer all questions fully and honestly.

2. During this period of training period, the slave agrees to obey Master to the best of the slave's ability and to devote herself/herself entirely to Master's pleasure, whether through readings, writings, dress, personal service or sexual service. This slave also renounces all rights to his/her own pleasure, comfort, or gratification, except insofar as permitted by Master. The slave agrees to learn what interests and excites Master through exploration and communication, and to incorporate such discoveries into this relationship.

3. Master now accepts full responsibility for this slave. This includes, but is not limited to, this slave's spiritual, social, emotional, physical and mental well-being. This slave accepts full responsibility for informing Master of all fears, concerns and anxieties on any and all topics, and also to inform him of any real or perceived dangers or safety concerns, whether or not they relate directly to him or to them as a couple. Concurrently, this slave recognizes and agrees that Master's decisions on any topic represent the

final word regarding the resolutions of such issues. The slave will not be punished for respectfully stating these concerns. Master strives to listen to slave concerns with a clear and open heart and mind.

4. The slave agrees to dress in the styles and fashions selected by Master, and Master does not make such dress requirements of this slave as to represent financial hardship or burden.

5. During this trial period, we will play by SSC rather than RACK rules. That is, the slave agrees to accept responsibility for using safewords or safe gestures when necessary. The slave acknowledges that the *physical play* safeword is **red** and that the *emotional* safeword is Master's given name. Master accepts the responsibility for stopping activities in progress to assess situations where the slave uses a safeword, and he will, to the best of his ability, immediately modify or stop the activity. The slave agrees to hold no ill will due to his decision. Master will not to punish the slave for the use of a safeword or safe gesture.

6. During this trial period, this slave agrees to use Master's given name, _____, as an emotional safeword. That is, if Master says something that violates an emotional boundary with me, I agree to communicate my hurt to Master by prefacing my comments with his given name.

7. The slave agrees to answer fully and promptly any and all questions asked by Master. This is a **FULL DISCLOSURE** Contract. Further, this slave agrees to **volunteer** any information that Master *should know* regarding this slave's physical, mental or emotional state. Master will not use this information to harm the slave in any way.

8. The slave has previously stated limits in a checklist and Master will not violate these limits without prior negotiation with and consent by the slave.

9. The slave agrees to address _____ as Master, unless otherwise directed. The slave agrees to abide by such Manual of Protocol as Master ultimately creates. The slave agrees to speak respectfully to him at all times,

including times not spent in a scene. Master may address the slave in any way he chooses that is not emotionally abusive.

10. Master will furnish the slave with such token(s) of ownership as he sees fit; the slave agrees to wear such symbol(s) at all times, except when he states to do so would be inappropriate or would non-consensually involve others.

11. The slave agrees not to have any sexual encounter other than with Master for the duration of this Contract and that the slave will not engage in self-pleasuring actions without requesting specific prior permission from Master.

12. The slave agrees and understands that minor infractions of this Agreement will be dealt with through *Correction* and that continued inappropriate behavior or material breach of contract will be Punished by withdrawing attention for a specified period and/or by administering manageable physical discipline in private. Any Correction or Punishment will end in debriefing and forgiveness.

13. If the slave commits an act that violates the trust that Master has placed in this slave, a third party (selected by Master if not mutually agreed upon) will be chosen to hear the issue and to administer a Consequence.

   • The slave agrees to abide by any Ruling made in such a case.

   • There will be a debriefing and forgiveness that will complete the cycle.

   • Time with this slave-in-training must not take away from established times with members of Master's Leather Family.

Fluid Bonding

Unprotected sexual intimacy is a very special Gift. Master will provide the slave with a hard-copy of his STD report and agrees that since that STD report, he has not had unprotected sex with any person outside the Family and will not have unprotected sex with any other person outside the Family while fluid bonded with this slave.

Fluid bonding with this slave may occur once these terms and conditions have been met:

- slave must test negative for all STDs in a test taken at an appropriate time after last sexual encounter.
- slave must agree that ALL future sex partners are **pre-negotiated** with Master.
- slave must agree that ALL future sex partners will use condoms during intercourse.
- If the slave lapses in striving for obedience, the slave will return to a state of obedience by immediately bringing this – like any other lapse – to Master's attention.
- In the event of an episode of unprotected sex, there will then be a period of protected sex between this slave and Master sufficient to enable this slave to be retested for STDs and to obtain test results.

Master will...

- Use the slave in any way he so desires, and for any purpose he desires;
- Encourage the slave to explore his/her slave heart;
- Serve as a Guide in the slave's quest for submission and spiritual connection through BDSM;
- Give the slave Directives and Instructions that may carry beyond their physical time together;
- Provide the slave such tokens of ownership as he chooses; and
- Correct inappropriate behavior in whatever manner he chooses. Such correction will end in debriefing and forgiveness.

Accepted, understood and agreed to this _____ day of _____

_____, _____.

_____, Master

_____, slave

Witnessed: _____

Dated: _____

Appendix B
The Safe Call

A safe call is a prearranged agreement with an outside party whose job is to call the police and/or get help if they don't hear from you by a particular time when you are metting socially with someone you don't know for the first time. It should be used any time you are planning a first meeting with someone. Often, it is used for second or third meetings as well – or until you feel you know this person reasonably well. This procedure can be used by anyone whether they are new to the BDSM scene or a well-seasoned veteran. There is a place for it even in the Vanilla world. *Whenever you use a safe call, be sure that the person you intend to meet knows that you are using this procedure.* It would be impolite for you to meet someone for the first time and – without letting the person know you're using these procedures – have to say: "Excuse me; I have to make my safe call right now."

Typically a slave/submissive/bottom set up the safe call, although a Dom/Master/Top may arrange them as well. Actually, either party can set up their own separate safe call. You gather all of the pertinent information such as name, address, phone number, driver's license number, itinerary, etc., from your prospective date and deliver it to a third party. You then set a time by which the third party must be contacted. If the call isn't made, then the third party calls the police, tells them that you might have been taken captive, and gives them the pertinent information

There are a few more details to a safe call. First, the caller typically has a non-obvious phrase or password to indicate that they are safe. This way, even if they end up being held hostage and are forced to make the safe call, they can still alert the third party. Second, the caller lets their prospective date know that a safe call has been arranged. The only thing that the prospective date should know is at what time the call needs to be made. (Be careful, time flies when playing. Set an alarm on your cell phone to remind you.). It should raise a red flag if the prospective date presses for more information and/or tries to dissuade you from setting up the safe call. An ethical person won't mind having a safe call in place – but remember: you must have notified your play partner that you're using safe call procedures. Third, YOU should plan to arrive in a seperate vehicle at least 15 minutes early so that you can park and get to the meeting place before your prospective date. You don't want this person to be able to identify your car or vehicle license number. Similarly, you should watch this person leave the area before you approach your car to depart.

Basic information is:

- Name and physical description of the person

- Drivers license number (you should have your prospective date fax you a copy of the DL – how do you know it is a valid DL number?)

- Phone number where you will be meeting or playing

- Address where you will be meeting and/or playing. (Playing is not recommended for the first meeting.)

- Type of location – home, restaurant, etc.

- When the safe call should be made (When meeting and leaving? Every hour on the hour with only five minutes of grace period? Etc.)

- A non-obvious phrase to indicate that you are safe. (e.g.: "OK, then put on your pajamas and watch a video, I don't care," means you're safe.)

- Any pertinent details on the meeting that you have arranged

Additional safety notes:

- Meet the first time at a restaurant such as IHOP™, that will have multiple cameras scanning the room. If you feel threatened, you can mention these cameras to the person you're meeting.

- The first time you play, (or... maybe even the first few times you play) avoid doing anything that may leave you unable to escape. This would include bondage activities, getting into anyone else's car, and so forth. You can save that type of fun for a later date.

- In this day of Caller ID, submissives in particular may have worries about talking on the phone with a Dom before they're ready to exchange names, addresses, and phone numbers (particularly when they have a listed phone number). If someone gives you a phone number and requests that you call, has Caller ID, and you don't block your phone number from being transmitted, he or she may be able to obtain more information about you than you could believe.

- However, your local phone company may allow you to block the transmission of your phone number to the next phone number (ONLY the next phone number) that you dial. Dialing *67 (or 1167 on a rotary phone) accomplishes that where I live. Try it out first with someone you trust, or check for the details about how your phone company does this in your local phone book. It may not be available everywhere.

Appendix C
Resources for Dress or for Formal Service

Books on Topics Related to Formal Service
The Art of the Table: a complete guide to table settings, table manners, and tableware. von Drachenfels, Suzanne. Simon and Schuster: New York, New York, 2000.

Butlers and Household Managers. Ferry, Stephen M. Booksurge Publishing: North Charleston, South Carolina, 2005.

Service Etiquette, Fourth Edition. Swartz, Orthea D. Naval Institute Press: Annapolis, Maryland, 1988.

Boots, Oil Tanned
http://www.stompersboots.com/gtwy_engineer-2.php#ENGINEER1

Equipment Cleaning Tips
http://www.purplepassion.com/purple-passion-hints.html

http://www.heartwoodwhips.com/info.htm

Men's Dress – "Outfits"
For "mess dress," I routinely monitor eBay™ under that search heading. This is an extremely reasonable way to come up with truly unusual dinner jackets, both US/non-US military services. If you end up desiring insignia and medals for non-US mess dress tunics, I highly recommend www.passinreview.net. The owner has been doing this for decades and has a huge wealth of knowledge. This is where I go for rank insignia and medals when my purchased tunics have come stripped. For US medals, see: http://www.usmedals.com.

Napkin Folding
There are some beautiful ways to fold napkins. These are among my favorite picks for websites that show you how to do it.

http://kitchen.robbiehaf.com/NapkinFolds.html

http://www.customlinenservice.com/napkins.htm

http://www.butlersguild.com/index.php?subject=44&nm=Napkin%20 Folding

Silver, Care and Cleaning
More than you ever wanted to know about maintaining your silver service, brought to you by the Society of American Silversmiths:

http://www.silversmithing.com/care.htm

Table Setting Choices
This robust site provides excellent photos and guidance about flatware and china placement as a function of the number and kind of courses being offered:

http://www.schonwalder.net/Tablesettings/list_a.htm

Uniforms
This is my favorite site for formal serving uniforms. My slave's serving uniforms come from here.

http://www.tipsuniforms.com/tips/catalog/index.php?cPath=2000_ 2700

For some FABULOUS maids outfits, try:

http://www.frenchmaids4you.com/Maids.htm

and

http://www.versatilecorsets.com/store/maids/page-01.html

Wine: Glasses and Serving Temperatures and Tasting:

This site describes every shape of wine glass known to man. Very impressive site:

http://www.diwinetaste.com/english/Serving.php

If you want to learn the correct techniques for tasting wines, try this site:

http://www.thewinedoctor.com/advisory/tastetastingwine.shtml

Wine and Food Pairing

http://www.butlersguild.com/index.php?subject=102&nm=Wine%20&%20Food%20Pairing

Appendix D
Travel Checklist

Trip Location: _____

People Traveling with Master: _____

Trip Dates: _____ Travel by: ☐ car ☐ plane ☐ other

Trip cash: _____ Credit card has $_____ available

ITEM	DONE
PREPARE TRIP FOLDER CONTAINING MEMOS THAT INCLUDE	
Name(s) of hotel(s) for each day, including confirmation #s and local phone #s	
Car rental information, if relevant, including confirmation #s and phone #	
"Weather conditions" report covering all travel days	
Attach a sheet that includes all relevant driving directions and maps	
If entertainment reserved, include all driving directions, times, confirm #s	
PREPARE TRAVEL SNACKS	
Teabags	
Powdered creamer	
Sweet-n-low	

Nuts, raisins, dates, apples, etc	
PACKING ISSUES	
Remove scissors and liquids from toiletries bag	
Verify that all pills are in the toiletries bag	
Ensure that we have an adequate supply of business cards	
Verify that there is a notebook and pen in the computer bag	
Pack snacks and liquor for hotel room plus shot glass	
Bathing suit	
One pair of socks and underwear per day	
Evening clothes: black dress slacks, dress shoes, black dress shirt and jacket	
Day clothing and shoes/boots – check with Master	
Jackets, rain gear – seasonal, depending upon weather; check with Master	

Appendix E
Sexual Stuff

Cunnilingus

http://www.howtohavegoodsex.com/tips_for_the_woman_receiving_cun.htm

Fellatio
http://www.sexinfo101.com/pm_fellatio.shtml

Good basic book: Tickle his Pickle; your hands-on guide to penis pleasing. Allison, Sadie. Tickle Kitty, Inc: San Francisco, California, 2004. www.ticklekitty.com

More advanced (and very good) book: The Ultimate Guide to Fellatio. Blue, Violet Cleis. Press: San Francisco, California, 2002. www.goodvibrations.com

Huge Sex-Techniques Resource Sites
These sites are particularly good about teaching stuff to guys about playing with their slaves sexually.

http://www.sex-project.com/1/

http://clitical.com/index.php

Pleasing your Master
Start with Jay Wiseman's books (Greenery Press: San Francisco, California): Tricks to Please a Man; and More than 125 Ways to Make Good Sex Better

Sex Positions
http://users.forthnet.gr/ath/nektar/kma/main.htm

http://www.sexualpositionsfree.com/index.html

An M/s Studies Book

166

Appendix F
Master/slave Conferences

If you intend competing for the International Master/slave title, you first have to win a regional title, then compete again at Southplains Leatherfest in Dallas in February. Here are the related website links.

"Feeder" Conferences

[Note: conferences are listed in order of occurrence after Southplains in February. Thus the Southwest conference appears last because it occurs in January – at the end of the competition cycle for the previous year.]

Northeast (Washington, D.C., July)
http://www.mastertaino.com/Master_slave_Conference.htm

Great Lakes (Indianapolis, August)
http://greatlakesleather.org/web/schedule.html

Northwest (San Jose, CA, TBA)
[Note, this is a new member of the M/s contest community. Their participation was announced at Southplains in 2006 and at this writing their website does not mention the regional conference.)
http://www.smodyssey.com/main.shtml

Southeast (Charlotte, N.C., October)
[Note – this event will not be held in 2006; check their website for updates.] http://www.togetherinleather.org

Southwest (Phoenix, January)
http://www.southwestleather.org

Culminating Event
International Master/slave Conference (Dallas, February)
http://www.southplainsleatherfest.com

Important Link
This link will enable you to identify all these websites at one time and also gives the names of current and past titleholders. Excellent historical site.

http://www.togetherinleather.org/MsRegionals.html

References

APEX ACADEMY/BUTCHMANN'S Protocol for slaves, Revised May 1998

Some of the material in this book was Inspired by and incorporated with permiss from SlaveMaster Mike McDade's "Principles and Commitment." Copyright © 1998 by Butchmann's Academy; all rights reserved. The material was used in parts of Chapters 1–4 of this book by express permission of Master Steve Sampson. To access this information in its original form, readers are referred to this link:

http://www.arizonapowerexchange.org/academy/protocol/index.html

Officer Wes' Protocols

I have used some material in this book that was originally created by The Good Officer. While it now lives on in a form and format somewhat different from Officer Wes' version, his thinking and writings nonetheless stand as the original material. You can find his protocols at:

http://www.westom.com/leather/protocol.htm

Master Gary McEntyre's Protocols

Master Gary McEntyre was kind enough to give me a copy of his own Protocol Manual. A number of sections from his Manual have been included, here, in their adapted form, principally in Chapters 1 and 2.

Service Etiquette

Some of the material in Chapter 5 was inspired by Service Etiquette, Fourth Edition by Oretha D. Swartz (Annapolis, MD: Naval Institute Press) 1988. There are many similarities between formal military dining protocols and High Leather dining protocols and I found this book to be particularly helpful in pointing out many of the details of such service.

An M/s Studies Book

About the Author

Dr. Robert J. Rubel is an educational sociologist and researcher by training. Immediately after college, he taught high school English in south-central Los Angeles for three years. Returning to graduate school, he earned an EdM in urban education and a PhD in the area of crime prevention in public schools. After some years working on staff and also serving as a Visiting Fellow for the U.S. Department of Justice, he formed a 501(c)(3) that specialized in research and training in the area of crime prevention in public schools. He ran that firm for 17 years.

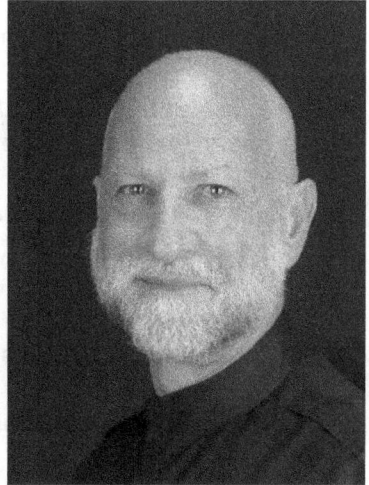

In 1985, Dr. Rubel formed the American Association of Woodturners and built its membership from zero to about two thousand in two years. At that point, the organization was turned over to people who had more time to devote to it. The organization is alive and well to this day.

In his mid-40s, Robert decided to change careers and joined a "boutique" stock brokerage and future brokerage firm in the Georgetown area of Washington, D.C. Within six months, he was made a Principal of the futures brokerage side of the firm and within another six months, named CEO. He ran the company for an additional four years. In the late 1990s, upon the request of a close friend, Dr. Rubel returned to Austin to help this person start a new company. He worked there as vice president for operations for five years, then retired to pursue his passion as an erotic and fetish art photographer.

Robert Rubel has been involved in the BDSM scene for a number of years, throwing himself into the literature of the field as though it were an academic study. He attends BDSM weekend conferences many times a year. Within his local community, Robert, (for the past two years using his professional photography business name of "Corwin") has served on the board of NLA-Austin, a Council Member of SAADE (School for Advanced American-Style Dominant Education), Director of SAADE's Special Interest Group for Master/slave relations, and for two years, part of the Leadership Core of the Austin Mentors Program – where he also served as a Mentor for fire play and M/s relations.

In 2008, Dr. Rubel was awarded the Pantheon of Leather's, Community Choice award as the "Man of the Year."

To view Dr. Rubel's erotic and fetish photography, see: www.photosbycorwin.com. ("Corwin" is the name that Dr. Rubel uses professionally for his erotic and fetish photography business. He also uses "Corwin" as his *scene name* in the Not-Leather BDSM community, in order to tie him to his photography website.)

To view Dr. Rubel's nature photography, see: www.scenesofbeauty.com

To review Dr. Rubel's presentations and calendar, use: www.RubelPresents.com.
E-mail can be dsirected to Bob.Rubel@yahoo.com.

While not a licensed therapist, Dr. Rubel is also available to provide informed guidance about your own M/s relationship. If contacting him for *that* purpose, please put the phrase "M/s Question" in the subject line.

Other Books by Dr. Rubel
Academic Books:
The Unruly School: Disorders, Disruptions and Crime from 1950-1975. Rubel, Robert J. D.C. Heath and Company: Lexington, Massachusetts, 1977.

Violence and Crime in the Schools. Baker, Keith and Robert J. Rubel D.C. Heath and Company: Lexington, Massachusetts, 1980.

Kink Books

Robert's books include:

- *Protocols: Handbook for the female slave (2006)*
- *Protocol Handbook for the Leather slave: Theory and Practice (2006)*
- *Flames of Passion: Handbook of Erotic Fire Play (2006 with David Walker)*
- *Master/slave Relations: Handbook of Theory and Practice (2006)*
- *Master/slave Relations: Communications 401 - The Advanced Course (2008)*
- *Master/slave Relations: Solutions 402: Graduate Studies in Meeting Challenges in your Relationship (2008)*
- *Squirms, Screams and Squirts: Going from Great Sex to Extraordinary Sex (2008)*

Three books of erotic and fetish photography:

- *Parts: The Erotic Photographic Art of Robert J. Rubel, PhD (2006)*
- *Wholes: The Erotic Photographic Art of Robert J. Rubel, PhD (2006)*
- *Holes: The Erotic Photographic Art of Robert J. Rubel, PhD (2006)*

To purchase any of these books, or to learn about presentations offered by Dr. Rubel, please see: www.RubelPresents.com.